A TASTE OF IBIZA

SHERIN KNEIFL
PHOTOS LUANA FAILLA

CALLWEY

CONTENTS

MONTSE

ZALATA
7ªIB-1-45391
7ª CO-1-83-22 IMAGINE II

FORE WORD

BY SHERIN KNEIFL

There are words that inspire dreams when they are simply spoken aloud. Ibiza is one of them, even for people who have never visited the island. But the Balearic island has the lot. Party destination? Definitely. Icon for dropouts? Absolutely. Natural beauty? Obviously. Hippie paradise? Certainly. Meeting place for the rich and famous? Undoubtedly. The list could go on and on, highlighting just how much these 571 square kilometers of land in the western Mediterranean have to offer. Ibiza awakens a different dream in every person, and manages to elevate their fulfillment into a matter of the utmost urgency. Reader, if you think this sounds like every cliché in the book, let me say this: If you think in clichés, Ibiza is not the place for you. Part of the island's magic of the island lies in its motto of "live and let live"—and that means every individual in their own individual way.

In the sixteenth century, Nostradamus believed Ibiza would be Earth's last refuge if the rest of the world ended. We are definitely not as gloomy as the famous prophet, and instead see things in brilliant white—after all, Ibiza is also known as "la isla blanca" because of its traditional white houses. This way of building uses local materials and is based on practical needs: Buildings whitewashed with limestone reflect the intense sunlight, keeping the houses cooler inside. Limestone was easily available and commonly used for both construction and repairs, As a result, Ibizan architecture is characterized by a sense of uniformity and considerably enhances the island's charm and appeal.

For the Phoenicians, who were among the first peoples to discover Ibiza, it was a blessed, fertile island thanks to its red soil, the fresh waters of the Rio de Santa Eulalia, the only river in the entire Balearic Islands—and its "white gold." Salt has always been one of the most important trading commodities and is traditionally extracted in Ibiza's salt flats in the southeast. The area is now a nature reserve and one of the most important salt production facilities in the Mediterranean. Its product, Sal de Ibiza, is bottled in popular ceramic souvenir jars and can be found in kitchens all over the world.

Fertility is an excellent keyword here: Tanit, the goddess of fertility and creativity, is hailed as Ibiza's protector, and her influence is also evident in this book. I'll take you from the bustling beaches to remote hiking trails in the north, turn night into day, and celebrate a lifestyle of mindfulness. As enjoyment is writ large here, I've gathered all the favorites, the iconic locations, and the insider tips, as well as classics and traditions. Because I've asked the people behind the fincas, beach bars, and garden restaurants for their favorite recipes, you'll be introduced to a kaleidoscope of the people who make Ibiza so unique.

Catalan and Spanish are spoken in Ibiza, and signs show the names of villages, areas, bays, and beaches in both languages. This book is divided into six regions, starting with Eivissa, the capital, followed by Sant Josep de sa Talaia (south), Sant Antoni de Portmany (west coast), Sant Joan de Labritja (north), Santa Eulària des Riu (east), and Formentera. It will guide you closer to your own idea of Ibiza as you read.

SANT JOAN
DE LABRITJA
SANT ANTONI
DE PORTMANY
SANTA
EULÀRIA
DES RIU
EIVISSA
SANT JOSEP
DE SA
TALAIA

IBIZA

SALVAJE BELLEZA

At the end of the 1960s, Ibiza was the hippest place in Europe. To be honest, it has never lost that feeling every summer since then. Vacationing on the island simply never goes out of style—and there are countless reasons for that, including the hospitable welcome. When the hippies arrived, they brought the desire for healthy "slow food," as natural as possible; the party crowd in the 80s sparked the opening of bars and legendary clubs; the wealthy international tourists in the 2000s encouraged gourmet restaurants—and the second homes of the dropouts and newcomers were accompanied by unique local concepts and hotels that now mix tradition with cosmopolitanism. All on a foundation of superb fish and seafood, meat and rice specialties, and home-grown vegetables, liberally seasoned with Sal de Ibiza and local herbs. On Ibiza trends may come and go, but good taste is timeless.

EIVISSA

Ibiza Town

The cathedral towers protectively above Dalt Vila.

EIVISSA
Ibiza Town

Ibiza's capital shares the same name as the main island. Ibiza Town, or Eivissa in Catalan, is probably one of the most fascinating places in the Balearics. Perhaps because of the laid-back way in which the 50,000 locals (more than a third of the island's permanent residents) go about their daily lives. Or perhaps it's the neighborhoods where few tourists venture and which are charmingly "normal" as a result, filled with market halls, hair salons, and barbershops, bakeries, stationery stores, tapas bars, and general stores? Or is it because of Dalt Vila, the "high city" that breathes history and became a UNESCO World Heritage site in 1999? Although the area—surrounded by a massive fortress wall, the Acropolis—dates back to the Phoenicians, Carthaginians, Romans, Arabs, and Catalans all left their mark too. At the very top, the impressive cathedral towers as if still watching over the welfare of the town. Next door has been a huge construction site for a luxury hotel in the state-run Paradores chain for years, but it's rumored the endless delays will be over soon and the doors to the 66 magnificent rooms will finally open.

Or maybe it's the old harbor, which gets a facelift every spring? Or perhaps it's the countless restaurants and little bars in the old town, all different, but mainly great? And then there's the mix of drifters, free spirits, and creative minds ... The list could go on forever.

This port city on the southeast coast is legendary. Unfortunately, the cruise companies know it too. Every day in summer, their vast all-inclusive ships disgorge their human cargo from for a few hours of shore leave, only to scoop them up again in the evening and sail onward. Fortunately there are plenty of sights worth seeing, so the crowds don't get in each other's way too often. The best way to escape the hustle and bustle is to take a traditional siesta and stay home, in your hotel, or on the beach during the heat of the afternoon.

Generally, the streets of Ibiza are thronged with a distinctly international crowd peppered with VIPs and celebrities. The old town and the Marina Botafoch are particularly popular, but true Ibizans only venture there to jog.

The buzz of summer evenings in the streets of the old town.

Flower power with added sparkle.

Cafés and bars on every corner.

BEACHOUSE IBIZA

THE GOOD LIFE

BEACHOUSE
PLATJA D'EN BOSSA
07817 SANT JORDI
DE SES SALINES
+ 34 971 396 858
beachouseibiza.com

A

A day by the sea starts at Beachhouse on Platja d'en Bossa at 9:30 am, with the flowing rhythm of sun salutations and a range of yoga classes. This gentle start wakes up body, mind, and soul—but also whets the appetite. Yogis and yoginis make sure to accompany their class with an order of coffee and juice from the breakfast menu, plus a tartine on rye with sunflower seeds or a bowl of chia pudding, say, mixed berries, and a dollop of agave syrup.

The best way to enjoy Beachouse is with good friends. It's a lovely spot that makes everyone instantly feel more at ease. Eating, swimming, relaxing, dancing, laughing, drinking … "Beachouse is our idea of what the good life means," say the owners. A mindful lifestyle includes favorite dishes that are designed to be shared. In fact, the restaurant is all about the "art of sharing," and while the menu changes from morning to lunch to dinner, the healthy Mediterranean focus stays the same. Feeling hungry? Lunch (1 pm to 6 pm) or dinner (7 pm to 11 pm) can be "small bites for the table," appetizers enhanced with more substantial choices such as a trio of tartare—red tuna, sea bass, and beef—followed by grilled salad with Comté cheese or sweet-and-sour Pyrenean chicken. Shared desserts can be flirty or fun, depending on the mood. No matter whether it's coconut with mango sorbet, chocolate fondant with salted caramel, or mini ice cream pops that inspires light-hearted, affectionate squabbling—everything is devoured in no time.

Seeking to make a memory that lasts longer than a full stomach? Check out the Souk boutique, part of the Beachouse resort, which offers jewelry and clothing made by eco-conscious artists. Every piece is inspired by a journey, with Ibiza as its stopover.

Left – Grilled seafood is showcased on the menu at this lively beach restaurant.

Below – From breakfast to sunset, guests are in good hands here.

Bottom – The experienced restaurant trio (from left): Brian Olocco, Sergio Cardeñosa, and Gennaro Vito.

GRILLED FORMENTERA LOBSTER WITH YUZU SAUCE

SERVES 2
DIFFICULTY

YUZU BUTTER SAUCE
175 g/6 oz shallots
125 g/4½ oz butter
50 g/2 oz brown sugar
50 ml/3 tbsp brandy
250 ml/1 cup yuzu juice
25 g/1 oz ginger
25 g/1 oz fermented lemon
Salt and Sichuan pepper

LOBSTER
1.3–1.5 kg/3–3½ lb. Formentera lobster
Extra-virgin olive oil
Salt

1 For the yuzu butter sauce, chop the shallots and melt half the butter in a pan. Sauté the shallots until soft, add the sugar, and let it dissolve. Deglaze with brandy and let the alcohol evaporate. Add the yuzu juice and grate in the ginger. Chop the fermented lemon and add to the pan. Season with salt and Sichuan pepper and let the sauce infuse for a few minutes. Remove from the heat, stir in the rest of the butter, and keep warm.

2 Halve the lobster, salt, and drizzle with olive oil. Grill it cut side down over charcoal for about 3 minutes. Turn it over, brush with a third of the yuzu butter sauce, and grill for another 3–4 minutes.

3 Serve the lobster on a wooden board with the remaining yuzu butter sauce on the side.

GNOCCHI WITH SHIITAKE

SERVES 6
DIFFICULTY

150 g/6 oz red onions
Extra-virgin olive oil
80 g/3 oz truffle paste
500 g/2 cups plant-based cream
15 g/½ oz garlic
300 g/11 oz shiitake mushrooms
100 g/3½ oz butter
Cayenne pepper
2 sprigs of rosemary
1 kg/2 lb gnocchi
10 g black truffle
Chili oil
50 g/2 oz grated Parmigiano Reggiano (aged 24 months)
Salt

1 Chop the onions and sauté in hot oil in a pan. Once soft, add the truffle paste and plant-based cream, then reduce by half over low heat. Set aside and keep warm.

2 Chop the garlic and shiitake mushrooms. Melt the butter in a separate pan and lightly brown the garlic. Season with cayenne pepper, add the shiitake mushrooms and sauté. Add the truffle sauce and 1 sprig of rosemary, and keep warm.

3 Meanwhile, cook the gnocchi in boiling salted water until they float to the surface, then drain and stir into the sauce. Let stand for a few minutes and season with salt.

4 Tip the gnocchi into a large serving bowl, shave the truffle over the top, and drizzle with chili oil. Serve garnished with rosemary and parmesan.

CALA BONITA

GOOD THINGS TO ENJOY

CALA BONITA
PLAYA DE S'ESTANYOL
07840 SANTA EULALIA DEL RIO
+34 605 450 592
calabonita.com

The chiringuito—which originally means "beach bar" or "snack shack"—is named after the bay where it nestles. Some determination is needed to find Cala Bonita; still a hidden gem, it is only reachable by a secret gravel road. The charm of this beach restaurant is all about a combination of two things: "simple" and "star quality." The vibe is casual, with rattan chairs and wooden tables on the bright terrace, but the guest list is packed with stars making reservations in the early afternoon for themselves and their cronies: top-league soccer players, jetsetters, musicians, and models. The crowd is often as beautiful as the place itself—*Cala Bonita* translates as "beautiful bay."

The menu has plenty to make a carefree afternoon perfect. There's always a new, creative salad to discover, with the Ibiza-style version as a perennial bestseller. The catch of the day varies, but is always grilled. The quickly seared tuna, served in bite-sized pieces, is a must. *Mules* (mussels) in a flavorful broth, grilled avocado, and sea bass carpaccio with citrus, pomegranate, and mint are other favorites. The professionally run bar serves up the perfect cocktails or a *limonada fresca* (fresh lemonade); on my last visit, it was passion fruit flavor.

So there are plenty of good things to enjoy on a visit to Cala Bonita. Stay awhile and swim across the bay before you head home—it's the perfect way to wrap up a wonderful time.

Far left – The grilled octopus is meltingly tender poetry on a plate.

Left – Jorge Manuel Ramirez is at the helm in the open kitchen.

Below – The restaurant on the beautiful bay lives up to its name.

IBIZA-STYLE SALAD

SERVES 2
DIFFICULTY
✹ ☼ ☼

70 g/3 oz potato
100 g/4 oz Ibiza tomatoes
40 g/1½ oz white onions
½ sweet Italian pepper
20 g/1 oz Kalamata olives
1 can anchovies in oil
3–4 slices (white) bread
6 tbsp extra virgin olive oil
2 tbsp sherry vinegar
Salt and pepper

1 Boil the potato until soft but not disintegrating. Quarter the tomatoes, cut the onion and pepper into julienne strips, pit and halve the olives. Place everything in a bowl.

2 Cut all but one of the anchovies into pieces and add to the bowl, reserving the oil. Cut the bread into 1 cm/½ inch cubes and moisten with some of the anchovy oil. Place on a sheet pan and roast in the oven at 180°C/350°F for about 10 minutes, then add to the vegetables.

3 Mix the olive oil and sherry vinegar vigorously into a smooth vinaigrette.

4 Season the salad with salt and pepper and drizzle with the vinaigrette. Mix well and serve in your prettiest bowl, garnished with the remaining anchovy.

GRILLED AVOCADO WITH RAW TUNA

SERVES 1
DIFFICULTY ✹ ✺ ✺

1 avocado
Extra-virgin olive oil
80 g/3½ oz red tuna
1 lime
1 radish
Chives
Maldon salt

1 Cut the avocado in half lengthwise and remove the pit. Sprinkle the cut sides with salt and drizzle with olive oil. Grill the avocado halves on both sides, then scoop them whole out of the skin with a spoon.

2 Cut the tuna into 0.5 cm/¼ inch cubes and mix with olive oil, lime zest, lime juice, and salt in a bowl. Set aside for plating.

3 Fill the avocado halves with the tuna mixture and arrange in a shallow bowl. Slice the radish thinly, chop the chives, and scatter both on top. Serve drizzled with olive oil.

LA GAIA

ART ON A PLATE

LA GAIA
IBIZA GRAN HOTEL
PASEO JUAN CARLOS I, 17
07800 IBIZA
+34 971 806 806
laigaiaibiza.com

It's impossible not to be curious about all of the plaudits collected by the Ibiza Gran Hotel over the years in the form of compliments and awards. The impressive building at the marina has an aura that has been attracting international guests since 2008. And it certainly has plenty to offer. In the lobby, the only limit seems to be set by the soaring ceiling. The elegant suites have views all the way to the old town. In the hotel's own open spa world and gym, body culture is on the agenda: Training for biceps, shoulders, back, legs, and butt is followed by hydrotherapy, the hammam, and the ice lounge. After all that, guests are ready for the casino and Club Chinois, the glamorous backdrop for the game of life. And art is everywhere; guests can discover the 400-piece collection on a guided tour.

So far, so good. But it gets better. The Ibiza Gran Hotel is reknowned for its gastronomy. Downtown Ibiza by Guiseppe Cipriani serves Italian dishes, while innovative open-air restaurant Zuma is inspired by the informal Japanese izakaya style, with its small, delicious plates. The jewel, however, is La Gaia by Óscar Molina, a restaurant that shines far and wide. It's as sustainable as it is spectacular, and has earned a Michelin star for good reason. Every plate is a work of art, every dish a poem. But before I get carried away with descriptions, you simply must reserve a table to experience its sophistication for yourself.

Óscar Molina takes a highly creative approach to Mediterranean cuisine, combining the best seasonal ingredients Ibiza has to offer with contemporary influences. His creations are full of contrasts and executed with the utmost precision. Molina's environmental awareness always shines through, imbued with a great deal of imagination.

Sommelier Vasili Abodzich enhances the experience, recommending exquisite wines. After refurbishment over the winter of 2024/25, La Gaia will continue meeting the highest standards and garnering acclaim in the new season.

Left – The art collection of the Ibiza Gran Hotel extends to the walls in La Gaia.

Below – Simply magnificent and utterly unforgettable: the table setting for a Michelin-starred dinner.

Bottom – Óscar Molina lives out his passion in the creative kitchen.

PICKLED LEEK AND SEAWEED

SERVES 1
DIFFICULTY
✹✹✹

MARINADE
200 ml/scant cup white wine
5 g/1 tsp pink peppercorns
5 g/1 tsp star anise
2 g/½ tsp dried bay leaves
5 g/1 tsp white peppercorns
2 g/½ tsp green cardamom pods
2 g/½ tsp star anise
600 ml/2½ cups mild olive oil
200 ml/scant cup white wine vinegar

PICKLED LEEK
3 kg/6 lb leek
800 ml/generous 3¼ cups marinade
5 yakinori sheets (roasted seaweed sheets, preferably Takaokaya brand)

PICKLED LEEK FOAM
30 g/1 oz glycol soda
250 ml/1 cup marinade

TO SERVE
120 g/4 oz pickled leek
30 ml/⅛ cup pickled leek foam
5 ml/1 tsp marinade
Hibiscus salt (Ibizan product, also available online)
A pinch of spirulina powder
1 pansy blossom

1 **MARINADE**
Reduce the wine to half its volume. Add the spices and oil and infuse for 30 minutes on low heat. The mixture should get no hotter than 70°C/160°F. Finally, add the vinegar and set the marinade aside for cooking the leek.

2 **PICKLED LEEK**
Peel the leeks to a diameter of 1 cm and braise in the marinade in a pan until tender. Remove from the pan and dry with paper towels. Wrap the leeks in the nori sheets (cut the sheets in half if necessary). Roll the leeks into a cylinder of 5–6pieces and wrap tightly in another nori sheet. Chill.

3 **PICKLED LEEK FOAM**
Put the ingredients in a saucepan and slowly heat to a max of 60°C/140°F. Pour into a siphon and keep at room temperature.

4 **TO SERVE**
Cut the leek into 1 cm slices and heat in the microwave for 20 seconds. Pipe a small amount of pickled leek foam from the siphon onto a plate and place the leek cylinder on top. Season with the marinade and hibiscus salt, sprinkle with spirulina powder, and garnish with pansy petals to serve.

Right – Bartender Roberto is the go-to for night owls.

Far right – The wine tastes especially good in the comfortable atmosphere.

Below – The bar in Ibiza's old town serves sophisticated cocktails and delicious small plates.

ROOM SERVICE IBIZA

MIXOLOGY

ROOM SERVICE IBIZA
CARRER DEL PASSADIS 10
07800 EIVISSA
@roomserviceibiza

Sought-after fashion photographer usually live out of a suitcase; hotel rooms in major cities are their second home. Perhaps that's why Riccardo Vimercati, responsible for numerous cover shoots for *Elle magazine* and advertising campaigns for Carrera and Calzedonia, named his bar and restaurant Room Service. In any case, the little restaurant in the old town looks magnificent. When Riccardo founded Room Service with bartender Roberto Rossi and entrepreneur Andrea Greci, Ibiza Town gained a touch of Los Angeles, New York, or Paris cool.

But the magic is in more than the dazzling appearance; the concept, pairing mixology with gourmet cuisine, is also enchanting. The menu is designed for a date night: fluffy homemade focaccia with thin slices of Jamón Iberico, toast with beef tartare, caper mayonnaise, and Parmigiano Reggiano, and a juicy, melt-in-the-mouth carpaccio served with crème fraîche and blueberries are both sophisticated and sexy. What man could resist a beautiful woman biting into a taco with tuna tartare? And she'll certainly appreciate her partner's gallantry when he orders six different mini pizzas.

However, the food is actually rather secondary—guests flirt through the cocktails. The Japanophile, with gin, yuzu, apricot, and cherry blossom, is stunning. A delicate slice of apple adorns the Apple Galore, with sherry and apple aromas sparked by cava bubbles. The undecided can order a 404 Page Not Found for a blend of light rum, lime, and red wine. The Nutty Buddy's cognac and coconut water piques curiosity, while the C4, with vodka, pink peppercorns, and Earl Grey tea, is an enlivening mix. Puerto Angel whips up tequila, mezcal, orange, and coffee into an intoxicating combination. But let's be honest: the classic Negroni is, and always will be, the first choice.

This urbane bar is the perfect place for an enchanting evening. Decorative photos from Vimercati's archives depict models in designer dresses or as God created them. Let the night come, and end with dreaming away in a hotel room.

LOBSTER ROLL

SERVES 2
DIFFICULTY

✹✹☼

1 lobster (about 250 g / 9 oz)
30 g/1 oz mayonnaise
5 g/1 tsp sriracha sauce
10 g/2 tsp white cabbage
10 g/2 tsp red cabbage
Lemon zest
Olive oil
1 hot dog bun
Salt and pepper

1 Cook the lobster in boiling water for 6 minutes, then cool immediately in an ice bath. Remove the meat from the shell and claws and dice.

2 Mix mayonnaise and sriracha sauce in a small bowl and season with lemon zest. Finely chop or slice the cabbage and season with olive oil, lemon zest, salt, and pepper. Season the lobster meat with salt and pepper, and mix with olive oil and lemon zest.

3 Heat the hot dog bun in the oven, slice lengthwise, and spread with the sriracha mayo. Top with the cabbage, then the lobster meat, and serve drizzled with the remaining mayo.

C4

SERVES 2
DIFFICULTY

45 ml/1½ oz vodka
3 g/½ tsp pink peppercorns
45 g/1½ oz. Earl Grey tea
5 ml/1 tsp lemon juice
1 strip of grapefruit zest

1 Mix the vodka and pink peppercorns and let them infuse for at least 8 hours, or preferably overnight.

2 Place the Earl Grey tea in a teabag and pour boiling water over it in a cup. Let steep for about 3–5 minutes, then remove the bag and let the tea cool.

3 Strain the vodka into a mixing glass and stir with the tea, lemon juice, and ice cubes for about 10 seconds.

4 Strain into a chilled cocktail glass and serve garnished with a fine strip of grapefruit zest.

SA PUNTA

COSMOPOLITANISM 101

SA PUNTA
ES POUET DE
TALAMANCA, S/N
07819 IBIZA
+34 971 193 424
sapuntaibiza.com

T

Talamanca Bay is also an excellent starting point for an unforgettable night: the marina's countless bars and Pacha to the right, the sea straight ahead, and above, the sky studded with countless stars. The perfect setting for a great restaurant like Sa Punta. Combining three restaurants in one, there's something for every taste and every spontaneous mood.

Let's start on the top floor, where Patchwork provides a colorful backdrop for a magnificent array of Lebanese dishes. It claims the pioneering title of the first Lebanese restaurant in Ibiza. The lavish decor does not distract from the fact that the dishes, which are often shared (groups of girlfriends often opt for baba ganoush, hummus, and tabbouleh, while men's groups go for lamb kebabs), are a great base for cocktails from the bar.

One floor down, and we're in Asia. Ginger serves dumplings, tempura, honey-marinated spareribs with lime, tuna tartare, glass noodle salad, and spring rolls. Here too, the motto is "sharing is caring," and groups love it.

The ground floor is the most exclusive. The fine dining restaurant is modern, trendy, and international, which is reflected in the menu. Owner Rodolphe lets his head and heart guide him in drawing up the menu in tandem with head chef Diego Dechecco, who then executes it to perfection. Lobster carpaccio, sea bass ceviche with yuzu, wakame, and sweet potato, or buffalo stracciatella with anchovies, confit tomatoes, and hazelnut crumble are a first-class opener. Then a trip to Argentina (Black Angus rib-eye with spring onion sauce) or Japan (black cod with mirin, sake, and miso)? Whatever you decide, don't miss out on the creamy mashed potatoes—and then start to plan where to while away the night until the early hours.

Left – The house in Talamanca Bay is a magnetic attraction for everyone seeking to plunge into the nightlife after dinner.

Below – Raw fish served as carpaccio.

Bottom – Diego Dechecco is the master of his kitchen.

MACKEREL TIRADITOS

SERVES 4
DIFFICULTY

CUCUMBER CHILI WATER
1 cucumber
Juice of 4 limes
1 aji amarillo chili
20 mint leaves
1 bunch Thai basil
1 bunch cilantro
Salt

JERUSALEM ARTICHOKE CREAM
500 g/1 lb Jerusalem artichoke, washed with skin
100 g/3½ oz cold butter
1 tsp salt

TIRADITOS
600 g yellowtail mackerel fillets (about 1 lb 5 oz)
Fleur de sel

1 For the cucumber chili water, peel and core the cucumber and blend it with lime juice, 400 ml/13½ oz water, and aji amarillo chili in a blender. Add 3 ice cubes and the herbs, season lightly with salt, and blend again until smooth. Chill.

2 For the Jerusalem artichoke cream, cook the Jerusalem artichokes in water for 1 hour, cool, and peel. Blend in a food processor for 6 minutes on medium speed. In the last 45 seconds, add the cold butter in cubes and the salt, place the mixture in a piping bag, and chill.

3 For the tiraditos, finely slice the fish and arrange in a circle on a plate, leaving enough space in the middle. Pour the cucumber-chili water into the center and pipe 4 dots of Jerusalem artichoke cream around the edge of the chili water. Serve sprinkled with fleur de sel.

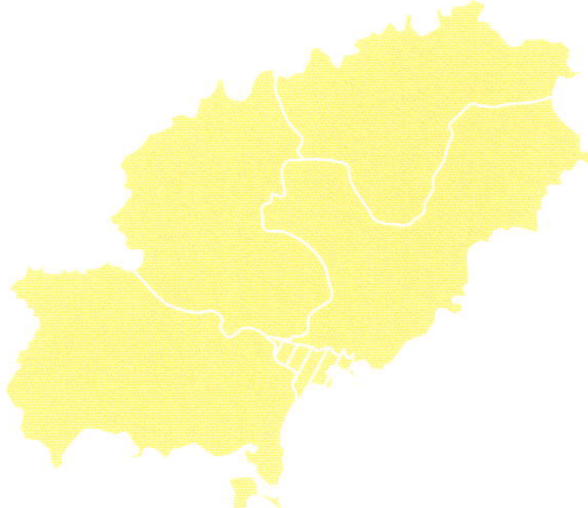

EIVISSA
Ibiza Town

1 LA TORRE DEL CANONIGO

A "small luxury hotel" with architecture that spans traditional and modern. The Mediterranean charm of the 26 rooms is matched by their luxury, and the spa services (massage, cosmetic treatments, manicure and pedicure) and El Corsario restaurant create comfort and well-being. Dine on the terrace while remembering Grace Kelly, Prince Rainier of Monaco, Salvador Dalí, Ursula Andress, and the members of Pink Floyd, who have also dined here.
latorredelcanonigo.com/en

2 VIVI'S CREAMERY

No tourist strolling through the old town can miss this eye-catcher in turquoise and white, with its long glass counter and the shelf of squat jars holding colorful goodies. A closer look reveals its focus on ice cream and sorbets with toppings. "Made with love," promises owner Vivian Rosberg. No promises, but it's possible her husband, ex-Formula 1 world champ Nico, might treat himself to a scoop too. Flavors range from tried-and-tested classics to creative ideas like rice milk chocolate with Hawaiian salt or New York cheesecake.
instagram.com/vivis_creamery_ibiza

3 TEATRO PEREYRA

After seemingly endless renovations, the legendary venue has reopened and resumed its crown as a cultural landmark. With an ambitious program, the island's social and cultural epicenter has a rich heritage. A great prelude is "Ibiza Hippie Heaven," a live show that combines music, dance, art, and dinner. Other evenings showcase the Pereyras, the house band. "It's our Cinema Paradiso, but with a happier ending," says the owner. We're happy to believe him.
teatropereyraibiza.com/en

4 ANNIES IBIZA

Anyone hunting for a dress for magical nights need löook no further than Annies Ibiza. These sexy dresses have also won the hearts of many celebrities, including creative director Giovanna Engelbert. The flagship store is located at Carrer de la Santa Creu 5 in Ibiza Town and is open daily from April to October. ***anniesibiza.com***

5 CODE

The renowned concept store has two branches that are a pleasure to visit. The main store is located in an old finca near Ibiza Town and brings together the casual bohemian cowgirl style that many visitors and residents of the island find so appealing. From clothing to leather accessories, jewelry, candles, and pillows, it is a treasure trove of attractive items. The second store, open during the season in the harbor area of Ibiza Town, is the perfect place for lovers of black, white, gray, khaki, or cream.
instagram.com/ibizacode.official

6 GEISHA ATELIER IBIZA

The tiny shop in Dalt Vila, Ibiza Townoffers tempting unique designer pieces from the creative owners, Kloshar (the hatmaker) and Sara Divita. The hats, rings, and women's and men's clothing all come together in a harmonious whole.
instagram.com/geis haatelieribiza

7 NOSS

A stroll through the old town inevitably leads past this bright shop with its inviting selection, which has been selling women's and men's fashion, fragrances, and accessories since 2010. Brands including Iro, Birkenstock, Asics, Common Projects, Moscot, and A Kind of Guise are artfully complemented by the store's own brand. ***nossibiza.com***

8 HOTEL MIRADOR

Within the mighty city walls of Dalt Vila, the 5-star Hotel Mirador is steeped in history. This Relais & Châteaux hotel is a classic with 12 elegantly furnished rooms and six suites. Breakfast on the small terrace is a delight, and dinner in the Michelin-starred restaurant is a gourmet treat.
hotelmiradoribiza.com

THE STANDARD 9

The cool US hotel group is a new addition to Ibiza. The white building on bustling Vara del Rey instantly became a hotspot, even for those who haven't booked one of the 53 rooms. The rooftop restaurant Up is the perfect setting for Asian-Mediterranean fusion, cocktails, and music, while the sun sets behind the cathedral and the last swimmers climb out of the rooftop pool. Groundfloor Jara opens its doors to beautiful strangers too; with its all-day menu, it is practically an extension of the lively scene on the square.
standardhotels.com

SANT JOSEP *de* SA TALAIA

SANT JOSEP
de Sa Talaia

Applause for the pilots when the wheels hit the runway is a thing of the past—Ibiza-bound passengers are far too cool for that—but the view that greets them once on solid ground is certainly worth applauding. Just look at those palm trees on the horizon, with the sea sparkling between them! The airport is in the municipality of San José de Sa Talaia, a perfect starting point for a holiday on the island. The municipality comprises five villages, each with its own personality and the right crowd to match.

The village of Sant Josep de Sa Talaia, as it is called in Catalan, lies at the foot of Sa Talaia, the highest peak on the island at 475 meters (1,560 feet). It looks like a traditional Ibizan village straight out of a picture book: the church forms the center and is surrounded by simple white houses that seem to have been cast into the center of the village like dice. Old men sit in cafés, occasionally whisperng to each other and earning benevolent nods from their colleagues.

In contrast to this tranquility, Sant Jordi de ses Salines is quite loud and bustling, especially when the flea market takes place on Saturdays at the old harness racing track or when countless day parties fill the beach clubs on the adjacent Platja d'en Bossa beach. The Ushuaïa and Hard Rock Hotel complexes, elegant Hï and SWAG stand out from the party crowd; the former has a reputation for being the number one open-air club and competes for supremacy in daytime clubbing until closing time at 11 p.m.

The time until sunset can also be whiled away at the beautiful Platja de ses Salines or Platja de Cavallet, which merge into one another, fringed with dunes and marked by the Torre de ses Portes, one of seven old watchtowers on the island. Mountains of salt tower along the access road. The precious fleur de sel is skimmed from the basins by hand and filled into turquoise ceramic pots. Ibiza salt also flavors potato chips or almonds, is enhanced with flowers or chili, and is one of the most popular souvenirs, evoking the taste of carefree vacation days in the kitchen at home.

The area also has a gem in store at sunrise: Es Vedrà, the legendary rock that rises majestically out of the water just a few hundred meters off the west coast opposite Cala d'Hort. Its appeal is magical, its history mystical. In ancient times, it is said that sirens sat on it and beguiled sailors with their singing; only Odysseus devised a strategy to avoid falling prey to them. Others believe it is the last visible part of the sunken city of Atlantis. Today, it is clearly uninhabited and calmly defies all speculation, but still exudes an irresistible energy.

All this takes us back to where we started: the first settlement on the island is said to have been established by the Phoenicians in the seventh century BC in the Sa Caleta area. Excavations only began in the 1980s, and the site can be visited today. Set against impressive red cliffs, the scenery provides fantastic photo opportunities to capture the moment for eternity.

The tranquil main town of the region of the same name.

One of seven watchtowers on Ibiza.

There are cliffs to hike wherever you look.

THE VIEW

PROSPECT OF A DELICIOUS EVENING

THE VIEW
7PINES RESORT
CALLE PUIG DELFGIN S/N
07830 SANT JOSEP DE
SA TALAIA
+34 971 195 200
7pines-ibiza.com/en/dining/
nela-popup-ibiza-restaurant

Even the journey there marks the beginning of a program of pampering. After collection at the airport, guests are chauffeured across the island to the west in a black shuttle vehicle. Open the tinted windows a crack. Can you catch the fragrance of vacation? Part of international luxury hotel group Hyatt, 7Pines is nestled in a pine grove and spans 56,000 square meters with gardens, pools, main building, restaurants, and numerous amenities. But the most beautiful aspect of this all-suite resort is the tranquility and the view of the Mediterranean.

It's no wonder the ambitious main restaurant is called The View. Executive Chef Óscar Salazar has been at 7Pines since 2024 and oversees a total of four bars and three restaurants. In the flagship restaurant, he blends his high regard for French cuisine with his appreciation of Ibiza's Mediterranean heritage to create culinary masterpieces. His dedication is evident in his careful selection of locally sourced ingredients, used in bold and flamboyant ways. Salazar has curated the dishes at The View down to the last detail. The menu thus becomes a personal narrative that regales guests with sumptuous epicurean stories throughout the evening. In Chapter 1, grilled leeks with smoked Mediterranean eel, peach, olives, and almonds rub shoulders with asparagus with dill, black garlic, celery, and white beets. An oyster with fermented strawberries and jalapeño also wants to have its say. Chapter 2 promises a harmonious team of sustainably caught tuna with beetroot, swede, and lemon, while a lamb loin with broccoli, smoked cream, veal sweetbreads, and pistachios also makes an appearance. In Chapter 3, apple, cucumber, sake, and walnuts depart only after the chocolate with almonds, chili, and mint has bid adieu.

If you can't decide, choose the tasting menu with four or seven harmonizing courses, also available as a vegetarian option.

Left – Executive Chef Óscar Salazar combines French culinary art with Ibizan products.

Below – There's no doubt why the gourmet restaurant at the luxury resort is called The View.

PRINGÁ MEATBALLS

SERVES 6
DIFFICULTY
✹✹✹

SOFRIT PAGÈS MEATBALLS
300 g/10 oz bacon
200 g/7 oz sobrasada (coarse, spreadable pork sausage, spicy or mild), or nduja
300 g/10 oz butifarrón (spicy, coarse sausage with pork and offal), or chorizo
2 kg/4 lb chicken legs
2 kg/4 lb pork ribs
1 clove of garlic
1 bay leaf
1/2 bunch parsley
3 cloves
1 tsp cinnamon
1 tsp pepper
5 potatoes
1½ pints/4¼ cups meat broth (preferably pork)
Saffron
Blanched chard leaves

PARSNIP PURÉE
600 g/1⅓ lb parsnips
210 ml/scant cup milk
90 g/3 oz cream
Salt

1 For the meatballs, coarsely chop the bacon, sobrasada, and butifarrón—this mixture is called pringá. Dry-fry in a large saucepan, remove, and set aside. Fry the chicken legs and pork ribs in the remaining fat. Halve the garlic and add it to the pan, season with bay leaves, parsley, cloves, cinnamon, and pepper, and fry briefly. Peel the potatoes and fry for a few minutes, deglaze with the meat stock, add the saffron, and cook until the meat is tender. Add the fried bacon, sobrasada, and butifarrón in the last 5 minutes and cook until done, then remove and stir together to form a homogeneous mixture. Remove the chicken thighs and pork ribs, strip and chop the meat, mix into a forcemeat with a little gravy, and shape into meatballs. Fill each one with the pringá mixture, then wrap in a blanched chard leaf. Set aside.

2 Strain the remaining broth and thicken it into a smooth sauce.

3 For the parsnip purée, clean and dice the parsnips, then cook with milk, cream, and salt in a saucepan until soft. Strain, saving the liquid, and blend the parsnips into a smooth purée, adding a little of the cooking liquid if needed. Season with salt.

4 Pour a layer of sauce onto a plate, halve the meatballs and place them on top. Serve garnished with a few rosettes of parsnip purée.

CANA SOFIA

LARGE FAMILY, LARGE APPETITE

CANA SOFIA
PLAYA CALA VADELLA,
CARRER CASTELLDEFELS, 10
07830 SANT JOSEP
DE SA TALAIA
+34 971 808 273
canasofia.com

Simply delicious is the conclusion after a hearty lunch at Cana Sofia. The beach restaurant in Cala Vadella, with its spacious terrace, offers traditional fare that tastes like home cooking, yet is so masterfully executed that it's clearly the work of a professional. The trendy term would be *comfort food*, food that fills the stomach and feeds the soul. The view of the sea is also Instagram-worthy, but faces stiff competition from the large plates and platters carried from kitchen to table.

They contain "thoughtfully simple" dishes, in the words of chef Moisés Machado. He and his team know how to cater to even the largest groups of hungry guests and ensure they feel well looked-after. Many Ibizans and holidaymakers from Spain book Cana Sofia for family gatherings, and paella is naturally the order of the day. The national dish takes on imaginative interpretations as a classic mixed paella with chicken, pork ribs, squid, prawns, mussels, green beans, and crab; as a house special, which combines seafood such as crayfish, shrimp, langoustine, squid, and mussels into a delicious symphony; or as the traditional and artistic paella arroz a banda, with grilled strips of iberico pork atop the rice.

I once spent the first lunch of a new year on the terrace at Cana Sofia. A good omen, because the year turned out just as wonderful as that delightful January 1st of oysters, tuna tartare, and champagne.

Far left – This lovely beach spot is open all year round.

Left – At Cana Sofia, Mediterranean hospitality and gourmet pleasures come together in perfect harmony.

Below – The terrace with views of the sea and the beach, where children can enjoy playing while the adults linger over lunch.

AIOLI

SERVES 4
DIFFICULTY
✹☼☼

Approx. 250 ml/½ pint sunflower oil
50 ml/3½ tbsp extra virgin olive oi/l
2 peeled garlic cloves
2 large eggs
Juice of ½ lemon
Salt and white pepper

1 Place a hand blender in a blender jug, add all the ingredients, and start the blender. Slowly move the hand blender from the bottom of the jug to the top until everything is emulsified into a smooth mixture. If necessary, add a little more sunflower oil for a thinner consistency.

2 Season with salt and white pepper and serve with bread, meat, or seafood.

CLASSIC PAELLA

SERVES 4
DIFFICULTY
✹✹✹

BROTH
1 stick celery
1 leek
2 carrots
1 rutabaga
1 parsnip
1 onion
2 cloves of garlic
1 whole chicken
500 g/1 lb veal bones
200 g/7 oz raw pork belly
25 g/1 oz salt

PAELLA
2 garlic cloves
1 handful of parsley
About 5 saffron threads
150 g/5 oz green beans/
1 red bell pepper
Olive oil
8 large shrimp (prawns), ideally red prawns
250–300 g/8–10 oz baby squid
300 g/11 oz high-quality canned tomatoes
1 tbsp sweet paprika powder
400 g/14 oz Spanish paella rice
or round-grain rice
16 mussels
Salt

1 For the broth, place all ingredients in a large soup pot and cover with 3 liters/6 pints of water. Simmer covered over low heat for at least 2 hours, then strain. Remove the chicken legs and breasts, chop the meat into small pieces, and set aside. Measure out 1.4 liters/scant 3 pints of broth and keep warm, allowing the rest to cool.

2 For the paella, first make the picada. To do this, blend garlic, parsley, and saffron with 300 ml/1 ¼ cup of cold broth and set aside.

3 Cut the beans into small pieces; deseed the pepper and chop finely.

4 Heat olive oil in a paella pan and lightly salt. Add the shrimp and cook briefly until translucent, then remove and set aside. Add baby calamari, chicken, beans, and bell peppers and sauté briefly. Lightly crush the tomatoes with a fork and add. Season with paprika powder and allow the liquid evaporate on low heat while stirring. The sofrito (sauce base) should caramelize, but must not burn.

5 Stir in the rice.

6 Add the picada (similar to pesto) and turn the heat to high. Pour in the hot broth and bring to a boil. Once boiling, cook for 8–10 minutes, then turn the heat down to low and scatter the mussels over the rice. Cover and cook for 5 minutes, add the shrimp and cook covered for another 5 minutes, until the rice is done. Turn off the heat and let the paella rest covered for a few minutes before serving.

If you do not have a paella pan, you can also make the paella in a wide, fairly deep frying pan.

SANT JOSEP

1 CASA JONDAL

Close your eyes and imagine the ultimate beach restaurant. Open your eyes, and make sure you quickly reserve a table at Casa Jondal. This utterly flawless location in the eponymous bay, a magnet for visitors, is as casual as it is trendy and is widely regarded as supreme—and supremely expensive. The quality, ambience, and clientele (models, millionaires, rock stars, designers, sports stars) are exclusive. But it's so worth it. ***casajondal.es***

2 MARIA B. CERAMICS

The graphic artist creates poetic ceramics that reveal the beauty in imperfection. Inspired by organic forms, the limited editions or one-of-a-kind pieces have an engaging character despite often being raw or austere. They can be admired and purchased at the studio in the salt flats, which the artist runs together with her partner, Argentine photographer Daniel Balda. ***instagram.com/mariab.ceramics***

3 EL CHIRINGUITO

The restaurant on Es Cavallet beach richly deserves the title of "the island's most beautiful beach hut." It has successfully retained the title for years thanks to its exquisite style, respect for the environment, and passion for hospitality. However, the term "beach hut" is a gross understatement for this iconic location. El Chiringuito's terraces are the place for perfectly grilled dishes, al dente pasta, and rice dishes made with local ingredients. A cocktail or cava sweetens the wait for a table, which you should reserve in advance. Afterwards, connoisseurs spend the afternoon on one of the daybeds on the beach, basking in the knowledge that "the sun is shining, the weather is sweet." ***elchiringuitoibiza.com***

4 JUL'S

This restaurant aims to be unforgettable for guests—and amazingly, it succeeds time and again, from the first step into the lined entrance hall to the trained staff. You'll find a glamorous dusky ambience, attentive service, and dishes which are a feast for both the palate and the eyes. Lobster risotto with pumpkin, espresso, truffle oil, and crispy buckwheat crumble vies for the guests' favor with the bucatini in a creamy sauce with crispy brioche crumbs, lemon zest, and beluga caviar. Shopping in the adjoining boutique, with its cool fashion and matching accessories, brings everyone together in agreement. ***julsrestaurant.com***

5 TROPICANA

The waves crash onto the stones, polished to roundness over decades. A place at the tables directly adjacent to the rocky beach feels like being in the tropics. Tropicana beach restaurant has been there since 1988, and is as inviting as ever for guests who appreciate good food. Although it is located on the glamorous bay of Cala Jondal, it has remained relaxed and intimate despite the occasional celebrity making an appearance. The menu features traditional Ibizan dishes, seafood, and international classics (pasta, sandwiches, fruit-garnished salads), as well as fresh juices. A place to return to again and again to savor the last moments of your holiday from a rattan armchair on the day of departure. ***tropicanaibiza.com***

CASA MACA 6

Imagine a retreat in the peaceful hills of Can Palau, brimming with authentic rural charm yet only minutes away from all the action. Lavender frames the main building, which proves to be a lovingly restored 300-year-old former farmhouse. Almond, carob, fig, and fruit trees provide shade next to the swimming pool. In the Ibizan dialect, "maca" means "beautiful." Very fitting for the ten rooms, whose simple design continues the natural theme inside. The restaurant also welcomes non-hotel residents. In the evenings, dining outdoors is common, usually with dishes prepared directly on the impressive grill. There is often live music or DJs playing chill-out tunes as the night comes into full swing. ***casamaca.com/en***

SANT ANTONI *de* PORT-MANY

SANT ANTONI de Portmany

Traditional fishermen's huts nestle against the rugged cliffs, surrounded by turquoise waters and Mediterranean nature.

But there's also sophistication on offer at this party destination in the west.

The west coast of Ibiza is the birthplace of chill-out, a music genre that emerged in the 1980s, probably to accompany the breathtaking sunsets. Even today, the gentle melodic sounds transport crowds of people to a harmonious world of the imagination. Audiences continue to flock to this natural spectacle, enchanted by the amber and red spectacle from one of the bars on the Sunset Strip until the fireball bathes the ocean rocks in color and finally vanishes below the horizon. The sea in the west is a paradise, shimmering—to stay with the color palette—from turquoise to Caribbean blue, with small bays and coves for swimmers including Cala Vadella, Cala Bassa, and the beautiful Platjes de ses Comptes beach.

San Antonio, the capital of the Sant Antoni de Portmany district, is like a British enclave during the summer months. Tourists from other countries need to be aware of this and enjoy it—it's a good idea to bring plenty of party spirit with you when vacationing here during the high season. However, there's no need to be put off: during the low season, the area is charming and peaceful.

Tranquility-seekers should visit in the off-season.

The lively resort and the town have a population of about 27,500.

Swim in the bays until sunset.

Right – Juan Torres helms a dedicated kitchen team.

Far right – The restaurant basically floats above the water, like being on a yacht.

Below – With its elegant ambience, the restaurant is ideal for special occasions.

ES NÀUTIC

MARINA WITH A MARITIME RESTAURANT

ES NÀUTIC
PASSEIG DE LA MAR, 8
SANT ANTONI DE PORTMANY
+34 971 341 651
esnauticrestaurant.com

N

Nautical science is the study of navigating a ship—in short, the art of helmsmanship. The kitchen at the Es Nàutic restaurant in San Antonio's elegant marina lives up to the skill and artistry of the name.

With its expansive terraces, huge windows, polished wood, and gleaming chrome details, the restaurant is a distinctive attraction. It almost feels like being on board a ship—in this case, furnished with a bevy of white-clothed tables, often arranged in long tables or large circles, so that entire families celebrating something can fit together. They order traditional dishes like bullit de peix—perhaps the most understated star of Ibizan cuisine. This classic fisherman's stew is served in two courses at Es Nàutic: first the chunky pieces of fish and potatoes in the signature sauce, followed by the rice, which has absorbed the intense flavors of the fish and is served in a pan for diners to help themselves.

The best-selling choice is rivalled by seafood platters, salt-crusted fish, and paella. The wait staff are as alert as they are skilled, their white shirts and navy blue pants adding the finishing touch to the nautical ambience.

Guests come to Es Nàutic for good reason, celebrating wedding anniversaries, a favorite aunt's birthday, public holidays. It quickly becomes clear why; the setting is elegant, but not starchy, the cuisine polished, but not pretentious. A place to let the hours pass by, flanked by gleaming motor yachts and sailing boats.

BULLIT DE PEIX

MIXED FISH WITH POTATOES

SERVES 4
DIFFICULTY

✷✷✷

BULLIT DE PEIX
2 cloves of garlic
3 tomatoes
1 bunch of parsley
700 g/1½ lb red potatoes (or any waxy potatoes)
200 g/8 oz green beans
Olive oil
About 10 saffron threads
1 kg/2 lb mixed fish (e.g., rockfish, monkfish, John Dory, scorpionfish, grouper in season), gutted and deboned

AIOLI
2 cloves of garlic
200 ml/scant 1 cup olive oil
1 egg yolk
Salt and pepper

1 Chop the garlic, dice the tomatoes, and roughly chop the parsley. Peel and quarter the potatoes; trim the beans and cut into large pieces.

2 Heat the olive oil in a large saucepan and sauté the garlic. Before it browns, add the tomatoes, parsley, potatoes, beans, and saffron. Sauté for a few minutes, cover with water, and cook for about 25 minutes.

3 Pat the fish dry, cut into large pieces, and add to the pan. Simmer for another 20 minutes.

4 Meanwhile, make the aioli :Place the garlic, 1 tbsp olive oil, egg yolk, salt, and pepper in a blender jug and blend with a hand blender. Add more oil until the desired thickness is achieved.

5 After a total 45 minutes of cooking time, use a toothpick to check whether the fish and potatoes are soft and cooked. Remove the fish, potatoes, and beans from the pot with a ladle and arrange them on a serving platter, top with the aioli, and serve.

6 Use the leftover broth to make arroz a banda: Brown 300g/10½ oz of risotto rice (ideally bomba) in a pan with olive oil, add the broth, and simmer over high heat until the liquid has completely evaporated. Serve in the pan after the fish has been eaten.

SEAFOOD PAELLA

SERVES 6
DIFFICULTY

✸✸✸

BROTH
6 cloves of garlic
1 bell pepper
1 onion
1 tomato
Olive oil
1 kg/2 lb fish bones
(preferably white fish)
1 bunch of parsley
Salt

PICADA
1 head of garlic
1 bunch of parsley
1-2 dried ñora peppers
1-2 peeled tomatoes
Salt and 1 tsp pepper

PAELLA
Olive oil
12–15 shrimp (prawns)
1 squid
1.5–2 kg/3–4 lb white fish
(e.g. grouper, dentex, monkfish)
1 bell pepper
12 mussels
12 crabs
1 kg/2 lb paella rice (ideally arroz bomba)
500 g/1 lb mixed ground meat
7 saffron threads
Salt and pepper

1 For the broth, crush the garlic cloves, chop the bell pepper, roughly dice the onion, and finely chop the tomatoes. Heat the olive oil in a pot over high heat and sauté the garlic, bell pepper, and onion. Add the tomatoes and cook over low heat for a few minutes. Add the fish bones, cook for a few minutes, and pour in 3 liters/1½ pints of water (3 parts water to 1 part fish). Add the parsley to the broth, season with salt, and cook over high heat for 1 hour. Strain and keep warm.

2 For the picada, peel the garlic and blend it into a paste with parsley, ñoras, tomatoes, salt, and pepper in a blender or mortar.

3 For the paella, cover the bottom of a paella pan or a large, tall pan with oil and heat. Fry the shrimp until browned, then remove and set aside. Cut the squid into thin strips and add to the hot oil. Cut the white fish into pieces and add halfway through cooking. Fry for about 3 minutes. In the meantime, finely chop the bell pepper and add to the pan. Fry for another 3 minutes, add the mussels and crabs and simmer over low heat. Stir occasionally with care, to prevent the fish from disintegrating.
When the fish is just cooked, add the rice and fry for 5 minutes. As soon as it starts to brown, stir in the ground meat and cook for another 3 minutes.
Add the picada, pour in 2 liters/4 pints of hot broth, and stir in the saffron threads; the rice should turn a deep golden color. Season with salt and pepper, lay the shrimp on top, and cook for about 12 to 15 minutes longer. Once the rice grains are no longer white in the center, take the pan off the heat and let stand for 5 minutes. Serve straight from the pan.

JUNTOS

REMARKABLY RUSTIC

JUNTOS HOUSE & RESTAURANT
CAMÍ DE S PLA, S/N
07816 SANT MATEU D'ALBARCA
+34 699 728 972
juntoshouse.com

It feels like a dream come true: Juntos House is perfect from A to Z. The renovated country house (set in plenty of land) is ideally located in picturesque Sant Mateu in the north. A charming wall mosaic by local artist Lucas Pereyra decorates the garden wall, within which the restaurant's terrace already extends The restaurant serves organic produce from its own regenerative farm, sourcing the rest from local suppliers. The owners give the farm-to-table concept a fresh twist by rethinking it every season.

This is reflected in the constantly changing menus: late summer and early fall, for example, feature sourdough bread with marinated olives and free-range chicken pâté, grilled polenta with carrots, hazelnuts, and blue cheese, and roasted cabbage with cashew cream, chili crunch oil, Parmesan, and buckwheat. The glazed scallops with celery and hollandaise sauce almost complete the meal— almost, because no sweet tooth would want to miss the muscovado cake with amaretto gelee, tonka beans, coffee granita, and almond ice cream.

The sign over the small shop attached to the house proclaims organic and sustainable products. Inside, hand-crafted accessories, delicate jewelry, woven baskets, limited-edition linen or cotton clothing for mothers, fathers, and children, and natural cosmetics and organic fragrances await their new owners.

Juntos House also aims to serve as a lively center for gatherings, which is underscored by a program of events featuring fascinating lectures and practical workshops. Why not take part in a gardening course or a cooking workshop and bring lasting enrichment to your life?

Left – Olive trees and herbs line the terrace, where moments can stretch into hours.

Below – Everything on the plates is sourced nearby.

Bottom – Pablo Fidalgo is an expert at creatively interpreting the farm-to-table concept.

LAMB SHOULDER WITH JUS

SERVES 4
DIFFICULTY
✹✹☼

LAMB JUS
500 g/1 lb lamb bones
1 carrot
1 onion
1 stalk celery
Olive oil
300 ml/1¼ cups port wine
Salt and pepper

LAMB SHOULDER WITH HERB SALAD
1 kg/2 lb lamb shoulder
300 ml/scant 1¼ cup lamb jus
2 bunches of parsley
2 bunches of dill
2 bunches of mint
Chardonnay vinegar

1 For the lamb jus, place the lamb bones in a large roasting pan. Roughly chop the vegetables and add them to the bones with olive oil. Roast in the oven at 200°C/400°F for 30 minutes until golden brown, deglaze with port wine and cover with water. Simmer on medium heat for 12 hours, strain through a cloth and skim off the fat. Reduce the liquid until a thick sauce is formed. Season to taste with salt and pepper.

2 Place the lamb shoulder in a vacuum bag, seal it, and cook sous-vide for 12 hours at a low temperature (approx. 57°C/130°F).

3 Preheat the oven to 220°C/425°F top/bottom heat, place the meat in a roasting pan, and roast for 20 minutes until golden brown.

4 Meanwhile, remove the leaves from the parsley, dill, and mint and mix them together in a bowl. Just before serving, dress with Chardonnay vinegar.

5 Slice the lamb shoulder and divide it among four plates. Pour over the jus and serve with the herb salad.

CHOCOLATE GANACHE

SERVES 4
DIFFICULTY

CHOCOLATE GANACHE
150 g/5¼ oz dark chocolate
150 g/5¼ oz cream

TO SERVE
100 g/3½ oz almond slivers
80 g/scant 3 oz cacao nibs
Maldon salt
80 g/scant 3 oz roasted pistachios
160 g/5½ oz dried raspberries
400 g/14 oz chocolate sponge cake
White chocolate powder

1 For the ganache, chop the chocolate and place in a bowl. Heat the cream in a saucepan, stirring constantly, to no more than a gentle simmer. Allow to cool slightly and pour over the chocolate. Leave to stand for 2–3 minutes, then slowly whisk into a smooth, shiny mixture. Allow to cool to at least lukewarm.

2 To serve, pour a layer of chocolate ganache on each plate and sprinkle the almond slivers on top. Add cacao nibs and a few flakes of Maldon salt, arrange pistachios and raspberries on top, and crumble some pieces of chocolate sponge cake over it. Serve garnished with white chocolate powder.

PETUNIA

NEW LIFE IN THE WEST

PETUNIA
CARRER DE SA PALA MARINA
07830 CALA CARBÓ –
SANT JOSPE DE SA TALAIA
+34 479 330 104
beaumier.com

G

Getting together and having a great time is what Petunia is all about. Located in a nature reservel, the boutique hotel in the west beautifully captures the atmosphere of the island. Following its complete renovation by Argentine architect and artist Lula Galeano and reopening in spring 2024, the redesign from suites to restaurants is a tribute to the vibe of Ibiza. Most of the 42 rooms and suites are delightfully simple and eclectically furnished with exquisite pieces—often 1970s-style furniture, individual works of art, and splashes of color (an orange sofa, a mustard-colored bench). They are scattered across *casitas* with bougainvillea in shades of pink, red, and magenta climbing up the balconies as if seeking to flirt. Many of the balconies, and especially the roof terrace of the main building, offer views of Es Vedrà, the legendary 400-meter rock off the coast.

The three restaurants are located in the center of the hotel and open onto the pool. Up-and coming Mallorcan Baltasar Rigo is the head chef of Petunia's gastronomic trio. He celebrates traditional Ibizan cuisine by interpreting it in innovative ways. Breakfast is served at Mesa d'Es Vedrà, while Los Olivos is the casual lunch option, and La focuses on **"CC"**: Dishes from the **crudo bar** (such as scallops in saffron marinade with quinoa soufflé and Wagyu tataki with plum vinaigrette and crisp potatoes) are complemented by decorative house **cocktails** (the spritz with tart herbal liqueur Hierbas and bittersweet grapefruit was a ladies' favorite during our visit). Live acoustic music often marks the end of the day and beginning of the night.

The other option is to complete the circle and have dinner at Mesa—yes, the same place with that delicious breakfast. Mediterranean dishes from regional ingredients are served as starters: marinated eggplant with Mahón cheese and spicy sobrasada from Pata Negra pigs, or tomato tartare with cheese ice cream, basil, and crispy yucca. The hollandaise sauce for the cauliflower steak contained a dash of port wine, with black truffle as the crowning glory. Velvety citrus and wood sorrel were the perfect complement to the cod confit "El Barquero." According to diners at the next table, the slow-cooked leg of lamb on a bed of pumpkin with glossy jus was divine. There was unanimity over the dessert: The tiramisu, prepared at the table from sponge cake, coffee, amaretto, mascarpone, cocoa, and the secret ingredient of pistachios, won everyone's hearts.

Far left – Freshly harvested produce from the garden; here, it's strawberries.

Left – Executive chef Balthasar Rigo and sous-chef Hector Hernandez.

Below – The spacious terrace awaits hungry guests.

SPICY STRAWBERRY GAZPACHO WITH TARTARE

SERVES 4
DIFFICULTY ✹✹✹

GAZPACHO
160 g/5½ oz pear tomatoes
130 g/4½ oz strawberries
17 g/½ oz cucumber
8 g/1 tsp red bell pepper
8 g/1 tsp Italian green pepper
8 g/1 tsp carrots
½ clove garlic
6 g/1 tsp sriracha sauce
13 ml/2 tsp white wine vinegar
60 ml/¼ cup extra virgin olive oil
Salt

TARTARE
8 red Ibiza shrimp (prawns)
(or other shrimp)
80 g/scant 3 oz fermented strawberries
Olive oil
Lime zest
Salt

GARNISH
20 g/1 oz preserved lemon
4 nasturtium leaves

1 For the gazpacho, blend all the ingredients using a food processor or hand blender until smooth or chunky, as desired.

2 For the tartar, peel, clean, and chop the shrimp, and dice the strawberries very finely. Season the shrimp in a bowl with olive oil, lime zest, and salt.

3 Arrange the strawberries on four deep plates using metal serving rings. Place the shrimp tartare on top and carefully remove the rings. Cut the preserved lemon into thin strips and use to garnish the tartare alongside a nasturtium leaf.
Pour the gazpacho around the tartare at the table.

SUCKLING PIG WITH CELERY PURÉE AND ROMAINE LETTUCE

SERVES 4
DIFFICULTY

SUCKLING PIG
1 Pata Negra suckling pig (or regular suckling pig)
100 g/3½ oz pork lard

CELERIAC PURÉE
160 g/5½ oz celeriac (celery root)
Olive oil

TO SERVE
2 baby romaine lettuce hearts
Olive oil
60 g/2 oz demi-glace

1 For the suckling pig, brush the meat with lard and place it in a roasting pan. Cook at 80°C/175°F for 10 hours, turning so it cooks on all sides, then debone and cut into 200 g/8 oz portions. Increase the heat to 160°C/310°F.

2 Meanwhile, make the celeriac purée: Peel and dice the celeriac, place on a sheet pan, and roast in the oven at 160°C/310°F for 30 minutes. Purée it with olive oil in a food processor or with a hand blender until smooth. Increase the oven temperature to 220°C/425°F.

3 Put the suckling pig back in the roasting pan and roast at 220°C/425°F for 15–20 minutes until very crisp.

4 Cut the lettuce hearts in half lengthwise and brush the cut surfaces with olive oil. Grill on the barbecue or on a rack in the oven at 200 °C/400°F for 4 minutes, then turn and continue cooking briefly.

5 Heat the celeriac purée and the demi-glace in separate saucepans.
Place 200 g/8 oz of suckling pig meat on each plate, drizzle with the sauce, and place a quenelle of celeriac purée alongside. Serve garnished with the grilled romaine lettuce.

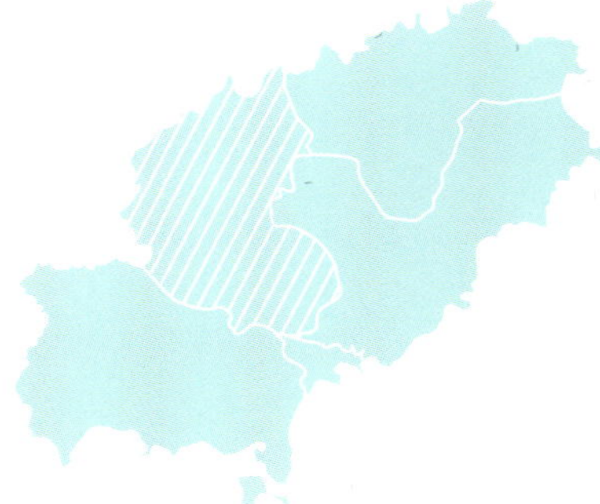

SANT ANTONI

1 SUNSET STRIP

The Sunset Strip is where romantics and party people stroll side by side. It stretches through the Ses Variades district from the harbor all the way to the small beach of Caló des Moro. When the sun has had enough of the hustle and bustle of the island decides to sink into the sea for the day, the views are spectacular. The explosion of orange, yellow, pink, purple, and red is the main event, but the music deserves the award for best supporting act. It all started back in 1980, when Café del Mar and DJ José Padilla created the perfect soundtrack for the natural spectacle. Soon, more and more sunset bars popped up to join them. The most popular cocktail changes every year, but mojitos, margaritas, mai tais, and sangria are always a hit.

2 SA CAPELLA

The atmosphere in the old converted chapel on the rural outskirts of San Antonio is special, making it ideal for special occasions. Why not spend the last evening of your vacation in this stylish restaurant, starting with a sundowner on the terrace? The menu offers an array of traditional and modern dishes, innovative creations using regional ingredients. There are plenty of starters to share, with raw dishes such as oysters, carpaccio, and tartare, as well as appetizers such as grilled clams with green sauce and fried Black Angus sweetbreads with citrus marinade. Curious to know more? You simply must experience the main courses and desserts for yourself, not to mention the friendly service, so be sure and reserve a table soon. ***sacapellaibiza.com/en***

3 ES TRAGÓN

Álvaro Sanz Clavijo earned a Michelin star in Ibiza, which has had a widespread impact. The culinary artisan relies on self-sufficiency (cured meats, cheese, bread, etc.) and a philosophy of sustainability, which gained him an additional green Michelin star. Gourmets can clearly taste the Mediterranean DNA in his avant-garde cuisine based on stews and slow cooking. The tasting menu offers impressive freshness, simplicity, and excellence. ***estragonibiza.com***

4 MADUNIA

At Cap Negret, a newcomer has made a sensational debut. The evening restaurant serves bold dishes that pay homage to local roots. Prepared mainly in the Josper oven or on an open fire, the dishes release their powerful flavors, with stellar examples of grilled salad with almond mousse and anchovies, potato tart made from thinly sliced potatoes with cream and caviar, and grilled chicken with lemon confit and aioli. Madunia translates to "Mother Earth," aptly expressed in the taste and feel of this cuisine.

5 CAFÉ MAMBO

What began in 1994 with an idea and a run-down finca on the cliffs of San Antonio has developed into a phenomenon. Music industry insiders mingle with tourists and locals to grab a spot at sunset and celebrate one of the legendary pre-parties together before continuing on to the superclubs. Steve Aoki, Fisher, Camelphat, Martin Solveig, the Swedish House Mafia, Carl Cox, Pete Tong, Boy George, and many more are regulars, veterans at setting the mood for the last rays of daylight and welcoming the Ibizan night with all its unexpected possibilities. Keep the feeling with an in-house radio station and online shop. ***cafemamboibiza.com***

6 O BEACH IBIZA

Life's meant to be celebrated, so a place dedicated to that aim just has to be fun. O Beach Ibiza claims that it may not have invented the pool party, but has certainly perfected it. The crowds of young party-loving barflies can confirm how great the show program is. ***obeachibiza.com/hotel***

7 IBIZA ROCKS

The No. 1 youth brand in Ibiza is one of the most famous destinations for music and day party tourism. 2,500 people (note: 90 percent British) celebrate exuberant pool parties at the heart of the hotel. Craig David and Becky Hill are residents. Don't need a break? Book one of the 362 rooms and stay on after the lights go out. But be warned: With a philosophy of "We never stand still, never stay quiet, and exceed expectations," you should be prepared. The most precious currency here is energy. ***ibizarocks.com***

HOTEL OKU IBIZA 8

The stylish complex has a peaceful location at the end of a cul-de-sac. But that's about as far as the "peace" part goes: at the head of the long pool is a DJ booth with video screens, children splash around in their own pool, and the spa and fitness program including courses and treatments is comprehensive and agreeable. To Kima serves ambitious Mediterranean-Asian fusion cuisine, while couples clad in stunning outfits enjoy Japanese delicacies in the evening at Oku. At night, they retire to rooms steeped in tranquility, with a decor of natural materials and earthy tones. ***okuhotels.com***

SANT JOAN *de* LABRITJA

SANT JOAN de Labritja

Every village has its church; the square in front is often used as a meeting spot.

A soap containing local aloe vera, a hand-stitched white linen shirt, a key fob made of colorful ribbons and bells, a ring locally crafted from ancient coins, or maybe a bottle of Hierbas, that notorious herbal liqueur made with Ibiza-grown ingredients? Tough choice. Best start by grabbing a coffee from one of the baristas at the Meke roastery, which has a booth at the Sunday craft market in San Juan (or Sant Joan in Spanish). Locals and tourists alike head to this little northern village to stock up on mostly handmade goods while listening to live music, chat with strangers, soak up a few hours of hippie vibes, and be inspired—like French designer Isabel Marant.

Sharing its name with the municipality to which it belongs, the village is not quite at the end of the world, but almost at the end of the island. The picturesque region in the north is known for its agrotourism hotels, which accommodate vacationers seeking peace and relaxation in picturesque fincas and often serve citrus fruits and vegetables from their own gardens. The hilly landscape is also wonderful for hiking, with routes of varying lengths and degrees of difficulty, ranging from leisurely strolls and easy walks to climbing expeditions.

The seclusion also attracts modern hippies who, like their 1970s brothers and sisters, celebrate an alternative lifestyle in harmony with nature and their spirituality. Bathers also feel at home in Cala San Vicente, just as they did in the 1970s. The bay, with its fine sandy beach, gradually deepening turquoise waters, and hotels with direct sea views, is reminiscent of Rimini in a bygone era.

You really know you're at the end when you drive the winding road to Portinatx. The island's northernmost spot sits at a dead end and is famous for its trio of beaches (S'Arenal, large and small, and Playa Porto) and its lighthouse. The Far des Moscater, with its black-and-white spiral pattern, is impossible to miss even in daylight. At night, the tallest lighthouse in the Balearics flashes a light every five seconds to guide ships. You could use it to find your way, too.

Picturesque scenes in the little streets.

Nature never fails to impress, time and time again.

Off to the beach with colorful gear.

AUBERGINE BY ATZARÓ

FARM TO TABLE

AUBERGINE BY ATZARÓ
SAN MIQUEL DE BALANÇÂT
07815 SANTA GERTRUDIS
+34 971 090 055
aubergineibiza.com

It's easy to see why Tanit, the goddess of fertility, is considered the island's patron. The garden at Aubergine by Atzaró is lush with burgeoning zucchini, tomatoes climbing up one side, and crisp carrots growing underground. Aromatic herbs are here in abundance. Proud fig trees converse with their neighbors, who bear juicy oranges. And in between gleam the eggplants that gave the restaurant its name.

The garden feeds the menu, which is dedicated to the farm-to-table concept. Dishes are therefore packed with organic ingredients, such as artichoke blossoms on tomato sauce with roasted garlic and Taleggio cream, sunflower seeds, and sunflower seed pesto. Acorn-fed ham and tomato on olive bread or a carpaccio of roasted eggplant with cherry tomatoes, feta, and pomegranate seeds are also great ways to start lunch. Continue with a millet burger with beetroot, sweet potatoes, leeks, peppers, and caramelized onions in an agave mustard sauce. Or share a main, add a salad (I recommend the pumpkin salad with feta, tomatoes, pistachios, black sesame seeds, and Dijon vinaigrette), and focus on the delicious desserts: cheesecake with mango and passion fruit, chocolate pistachio brownie with salted caramel ice cream, tarte tatin, or homemade pear crumble cake.

The three hectares of fruit and vegetables are as lush as the romantic atmosphere of the estate. It's usual to be seated outside amid all this splendor, but the finca's interior also has a welcoming atmosphere, in pale colors enhanced by olive green accents. Many a wedding or anniversary celebration has already hailed happiness here.

The Atzaró Group runs this charming rural restaurant on the road between Santa Gertrudis and San Miquel, as well as an agrotourism hotel among other activities. The estate embraces nature with understated luxury, extending over 13 hectares of paradise. Wellness in its literal sense is on the agenda here, right down to absolute relaxation. In addition, informal and relaxed Atzaró Beach blends harmoniously with its surroundings. The boho style extends across so many cozy areas that it's tempting to spend hours there. Whether inland or with a sea view, all the houses unite the quality to which these hospitable entrepreneurs are dedicated.

Far left – Don't miss the finca behind the big wall on the long road.

Left – Rosina Walter puts her heart, soul, and skill into the kitchen.

Below – The garden is wholly organic, the outdoor spot is utterly picturesque.

TARTARE OF ROASTED EGGPLANT

SERVES 4
DIFFICULTY

CHILI OIL
1 chili pepper
200 ml/scant 1 cup olive oil

4 eggplants
1 pomegranate
6 dates
4 tbsp balsamic vinegar
10 g/½ oz mint
10 g/½ oz parsley
24 cherry tomatoes
200 g/7 oz feta
1 handful of pistachios
40 g/2 oz arugula pesto
40 g/2 oz tahini sauce
1 naan bread
2 tbsp garlic-lime butter
Fleur de sel

1 For the chili oil, remove the stem and seeds from the chili pepper and place in a saucepan with the olive oil. Simmer over low heat for about 30 minutes, purée, and store in a glass container in the refrigerator.

2 Roast the eggplants directly on the stove top or on the grill, turning constantly, until the skin is charred and peels away. Then bake in the oven at 180°C/350°F for about 30 minutes on a wire rack until soft, remove and allow to cool. Peel the eggplants, drain the flesh in a sieve, and set aside.

3 Deseed the pomegranate. Pit and chop the dates, and drizzle with balsamic vinegar in a bowl. Chop the mint and parsley, halve the cherry tomatoes. Crumble the feta cheese, and chop the pistachios.

4 Place the drained eggplant pulp on four plates, drizzle with chili oil, and spread evenly with your hand. Season with salt.

5 Use the arugula pesto to draw zigzag lines in one direction over the eggplant, and the tahini sauce in the opposite direction. Then sprinkle the chopped herbs, dates, feta, pomegranate seeds, and finally the cherry tomatoes on top. Drizzle more chili oil, tahini sauce, and arugula pesto in a zigzag pattern over everything again.

6 Heat up the naan bread, spread it with garlic-lime butter, and sprinkle with fleur de sel. Quarter it and serve warm with the tartare.

TURKISH EGGPLANTS

SERVES 4
DIFFICULTY

1 onion
1 clove of garlic
1 bunch of parsley
1 bunch of mint
1 bunch of cilantro
1 thumb-sized piece of ginger
600 g/1¼ lb ground meat (lamb and beef)
1 tbsp + 200 g/7 oz Greek yogurt
1 tbsp honey
½ tsp chili powder
1 tbsp ras el-hanout
1 kg/2 lb strained tomatoes
1 tbsp tomato paste
2 eggplants
Olive oil
2 tbsp tahini
1 splash of pomegranate syrup
¼ red onion
100 g/3½ oz arugula
4 tbsp balsamic vinaigrette

1 Finely chop the onion, garlic, parsley, mint, and cilantro, grate the ginger, and mix everything with the meat in a bowl. Add 1 tbsp yogurt, honey, chili powder, and ras el-hanout, and mix well. Dry-fry the ground meat over low heat in its own lamb fat, adding a few drops of olive oil if needed. Once well browned, stir in the tomatoes and tomato paste and cook for about 20 minutes until the mixture is reduced and thickened. Cool.

2 Cut the eggplants in half lengthwise, drizzle with olive oil, and bake on a sheet pan in the oven at 180°C/350°F for about 30 minutes until golden and soft. Let them cool and scoop out most of the flesh. Fill the eggplant halves with the meat mixture and bake for another 12 minutes at 180°C/350°F.

3 Meanwhile, for the sauce, mix 200 g/7 oz yogurt with tahini and pomegranate syrup. Chop the red onion and mix it with the arugula and balsamic vinaigrette.

4 Arrange the stuffed eggplants on four plates and serve with the yogurt-tahini sauce and arugula salad.

CAN MARTÍ

PEACE SETTLES IN

FINCA CAN MARTÍ
VENDA DE CA'S RIPOLLS, 29
07810 SAN JUAN BAUTISTA
+34 971 333 500
canmarti.com

I can't deny this is one of my very favorite places on Ibiza. The reasons why I fell in love with Can Martí at first sight are as many as they are obvious. The best place to start is probably the picturesque location, because this classic finca, now an agroturismo, sits at the heart of a nature reserve in the north of the island. The main house and the equally distinctive outbuildings with their white-washed walls are surrounded by a 42-hectare/104-acres estate, all connected by a patchwork of organically farmed areas: vegetable beds, aromatic herb gardens, orchards, and an olive grove. Everything is grown using eco-friendly, sustainable methods, based on the principles of permaculture. Guests can sample and purchase the farm's produce, homemade specialties, snacks, and other delicacies in the small organic shop on site. Naturally, these products also feature in the eco-hotel's cuisine. "We believe that everything that is in harmony with nature is also in harmony with the human body. We then transform our produce, grown with care and dedication, into healthy, homemade snacks and meals for our guests," says owner Tom Brantschen.

The ideal way to start the day is with a few laps in the natural pool or yoga with sun salutations. Afterwards, breakfast tastes even better. The morning menu includes freshly squeezed orange juice, berries or other fruits with yogurt, while the eggs for the omelet, tortilla, or scrambled eggs with herbs come from the chickens strutting around the grounds. The coffee is locally roasted and the milk is organic. The daily lunch specials and snacks feature whatever is in season. Every Monday evening, Tom organizes a meal with freshly harvested ingredients from the finca. "Reconnecting with nature through your taste buds is today's luxury," he smiles.

The evening atmosphere is also truly luxurious. Guests returning to their suites after dinner under the stars are greeted with peace and quiet. Every piece of furniture seems to have its rightful place, the pale colors, terracotta tiles, wooden beams, natural fabrics, and white walls all harmonize. It's hard to find a more relaxed night's sleep. Unless one of the donkeys on the property gets bored and brays loudly for attention, briefly shattering the perfect peace.

Far left – The decor reflects the rural idyll. Lunch is also a seamless fit.

Left – Chef Samuel Schneider (left) and owner Tom Brantschen.

Below – The finca's guest houses and dining options are spread across several buildings on the property.

SEA BASS WITH SWEET POTATO AND CRISPY KALE

SERVES 2
DIFFICULTY
✹☼☼

1 large sweet potato
2 sea bass fillets with skin, deboned
Olive oil
Sage
500 g/1 lb kale
Sage-infused olive oil optional)
Fleur de sel

1 Wash the sweet potato well, sprinkle with fleur de sel, wrap it in aluminum foil and roast in the oven at 180°C/350°F for about 50 minutes.

2 Meanwhile, season the fish fillets with olive oil, sage leaves, and salt.

3 Wash the kale, strip the stalks from the leaves with a knife and discard the stalks. Roughly chop the tender leaves, mix with olive oil and salt, and bake on a parchment-lined sheet pan at 190 °C/375°F for 5 minutes or until crisp.

4 Heat olive oil in a pan and sear the fish fillets skin-side down over medium heat. After about 2 minutes, cover the pan and cook for 7 minutes.

5 Remove the sweet potato from the foil, cut it in half, and place each half on a plate. Top with kale, arrange the fillets alongside, and serve drizzled with sage-infused olive oil.

HOMEMADE TRUFFLES WITH RED FRUITS

SERVES 4
DIFFICULTY

300 g/10 oz dates, pitted
200 ml/scant 1 cup coconut oil
50 g/2 oz hazelnuts
50 g/2 oz cashews
50 g/2 oz cocoa powder
2 tbsp agave syrup
Shredded coconut
Salt
Red fruits (for garnish)

1 Mix the dates and coconut oil in a bowl and soak for 20 minutes.

2 Place the hazelnuts, cashews, soaked dates, and a pinch of salt in a food processor and blend until smooth.

3 Place the mixture in a stainless steel bowl with the cocoa powder and agave syrup and stir over a water bath until smooth. Allow to cool until the mixture can be handled, and shape into truffles with your hands. Roll in shredded coconut and serve on a small plate garnished with red fruits.

Right – Ben Shpunt (left) is in charge of the concept, Chardonné Cooper (middle) handles the wine, and Marci Mikola is responsible for the menu.

Far right – Natural wines are the passion of both the owners and the guests.

Below – Casual, without compromising on quality.

CASA LHASA

TRANSPARENT AND ETHICAL

CASA LHASA
CARRETERA SANT LLORENÇ, 2
07812 SANT LORENÇ
DE BALÀFIA
+34 971 205 893
casalhasa.com

One might think that the food at Casa Lhasa is merely there as an accompaniment to the wine. This would be an injustice to the unpretentious local cuisine, which is exceptionally skillfully prepared. Nevertheless, the focus of this charming restaurant in the village of San Lorenç is on natural wines, making it a favorite with those who appreciate a fine drop. Cassady Sniatowsky, co-owner of Casa Lhasa, is a sommelier by profession, but soon turned to natural wines because he was concerned by the lack of transparency in conventional wines. Together with partner Ben Shpunt, he founded the natural wine bar and restaurant, thus not only upholding the diversity and heritage of natural wines, but also providing a place where people come together to enjoy a relaxed atmosphere.

The ethos of their concept is a conscious focus on food and drink. The menu changes almost daily depending on what ingredients are available, most sourced from nearby farms to ensure the dishes are as seasonal, local, and organic as possible. There are plenty of vegetables, such as tempura zucchini with lemon mayo and beets with ricotta, walnuts, and vinaigrette. Meat follows a nose-to-tail philosophy, using creativity to maximize flavor: Pork head terrine with pickled dates, lamb shank with a rich jus, and oriental-style veal sweetbreads with labneh, chili, and sumac are excellent ideas that translate into imaginative results on the plates. The fish also comes from a trusted local fisherman.

The innovative restaurant is run by a passionate and curious team that lives and breathes authenticity. The wine cellar stocks products by hand-picked holistic winemakers, from countries with a history of natural wine production, such as Georgia and Italy, to those that have only recently devoted themselves to this art, among them France and Spain. The holistic philosophy is borne out by the rural charm—in summer, guests dine under the branches of the many fruit trees, and in winter, they cozy up in front of the fireplace.

BABY LEEKS WITH VINAIGRETTE

SERVES 2
DIFFICULTY ✹☼☼

500 g/1 lb leeks (ideally fresh from the market)
250 ml/1 cup olive oil plus more for frying
100 ml/scant ½ cup natural white wine vinegar
75 g/3 oz Dijon mustard
Salt and pepper

1 Clean the leeks, trim the top and bottom ends, and blanch for 3–5 minutes until soft. Strain and cool in ice water, then squeeze out as much water as possible.

2 Heat olive oil in a pan, season the leeks with salt and pepper, and fry them in the hot oil.

3 Whisk together oil, white wine vinegar, and mustard to make a vinaigrette.

4 Arrange the leeks on a serving platter and serve generously drizzled with vinaigrette.

HAZELNUT TART

FOR 2 TARTS
DIFFICULTY

TART BASE
500 g/generous 1 lb wheat flour
150 g/5⅓ oz powdered sugar
300 g/10 oz butter at room temperature
1 egg
2 egg yolks

FILLING
300 g/10½ oz sugar
250 g/9 oz butter
3 eggs
1 tbsp crème fraîche
300 g/10½ oz roasted hazelnuts
Maldon salt

1 Mix all the ingredients for the tart base to a smooth dough in a food processor, then cover and chill for 2 hours.

2 Preheat the oven to 160°C/320°F top/bottom heat. Grease 2 small tart pans, split the dough in half and roll out each half with a rolling pin to fit the pans. Place the dough in the pans, press down gently, and bake in the preheated oven for 10 minutes.

3 Meanwhile, mix all the ingredients for the filling in a food processor, adding the hazelnuts last. They should not be chopped too finely so that they are still noticeable later, so take care not to run the machine for too long.

4 Spread the mixture over the pre-baked bases, turn the heat up to 180°C/400°F, and bake the tarts for another 30 minutes. Cool on a wire rack before serving.

LA PALOMA

WHITE DOVE ON A SKY-BLUE BACKGROUND

LA PALOMA
CARRER CAN POU, 4
07812 SANT LLORENÇ
DE BALÀFIA
+34 971 325 543
palomaibiza.com

In this Garden of Eden, all are welcome—as long as they have a reservation. Otherwise, waiting can really test your patience. Once guests have snagged a spot in the shade of the orange trees, they are happy to spend whole afternoons at La Paloma. Fortunately, time is no big issue in Ibiza.

Imagine sitting at one of the colorfully painted wooden tables, catching the sun's shadows slanting through the leaves, and taking in the pretty little vases of flowers in front of you, complemented by plates with floral decorations. A slate board is brought over and leaned against a straw chair. On it, handwritten in white chalk, is the menu: stuffed focaccia with rosemary, goat cheese with caramelized nuts, falafel salad, crudité with variations of hummus, a white sourdough pizza, or a substantial burger. Chef Nir Cohen is part of the Paloma crew that runs the island's restaurant. In its family atmosphere, he combines flavors from the Middle East—his homeland—with Asian and North African influences, often using Mediterranean ingredients. "My aim is to cook traditional dishes while being innovative," he says. The results are a parade of fresh lunch dishes with "sunshine flavors." The limonada fresca also tastes of sunshine, and with mint and a pinch of chili over plenty of crushed ice, it can compete with any Aperol spritz.

La Paloma is a favorite spot that treats guests like family, whether they are a French movie star, a Dutch supermodel, a Parisian fashion designer, or a vintage furniture icon from Zurich. The sense of community is helped by the fact that the staff have stayed loyal for years. And what else is part of the family? That's right: children. They have their own little playground paradise, where parents can keep an eye on them from the garden seating area.

La Paloma was born 20 years ago out of a desire to create a restaurant in harmony with the beauty of the island. The owners started out small in a finca in the village of San Lorenzo. Now, the light blue restaurant with its white dove logo is an institution and an enchanting place that draws visitors back again and again.

Far left – Flavors from the Middle East meet Asian and North African influences.

Left – Nir Cohen runs La Paloma by Day.

Below – The garden is a small corner of paradise.

FALAFEL

SERVES 4
DIFFICULTY

250 g/9 oz dried chickpeas
2 medium white onions
2 tbsp coriander seeds
2 tbsp cumin seeds
7 cardamom pods
1 bunch of cilantro
1 bunch of parsley
1 tsp baking powder
Sunflower oil
1 tsp salt

1 Soak the chickpeas in water overnight.

2 Drain the next morning. Chop the onions and mince them together with the chickpeas, preferably using a meat grinder, or alternatively a food processor.

3 Grind the spices, finely chop the cilantro and parsley, and mix everything with the ground chickpeas, baking powder, and salt.

4 Shape the mixture into balls. Heat the sunflower oil to 180°C/350°F in a saucepan and fry the falafel in batches until golden brown. Drain and serve hot with fresh salad, flatbread, and tahini.

ORANGE ALMOND CAKE WITH VANILLA YOGURT

SERVES 6
DIFFICULTY

2 oranges
250 g/1 cup sugar
6 eggs
250 g/1 cup almond flour
250 g/1 cup Greek yogurt
2 tbsp agave syrup
Seeds from 1 vanilla pod
Orange zest
Salt

1 Boil the oranges whole (with peel) in water until soft, then cut them in half, remove the seeds, and puree the fruit whole.

2 Preheat the oven to 170°C/325°F top/bottom heat.

3 Whisk the sugar and eggs together with a pinch of salt and gradually mix in the orange puree. Stir in the almond flour and pour the batter into a greased 23 cm cake tin. Bake the cake for 45 minutes until golden brown.

4 Meanwhile, mix the yogurt, agave syrup, vanilla seeds, and orange zest, and serve the slightly cooled cake with the vanilla yogurt.

SALVIA

WITH HEART AND SOUL

SALVIA
CA NA XICA HOTEL & SPA
CTRA. SANT MIQUEL, KM. 10
07815 SANT MIQUEL
+34 629 676 781
salviaibiza.com

Drive from Santa Gertrudis to San Miguel and turn right about two-thirds of the way there. That's where you'll find the Ca Na Xica Boutique Hotel estate, looking as picturesque in the landscape as if Caspar David Friedrich and Vincent van Gogh had joined forces to paint it. In the midst of this idyll lies Salvia, designed for sophisticated guests with the most discerning tastes.

As soon as you arrive at the restaurant, all your expectations are overturned and you surrender yourself to the culinary experience in this place without reservation. "Our philosophy is based on the quality of the raw ingredients, but also on the simplicity, elegance, and sophistication of each dish. Once you understand the essence of an ingredient, its flavor can be enhanced through hard work, dedication, perseverance, and passion," explains chef Pablo Carrizo. The veteran chef trained at El Bulli, El Celler de Can Roca, and Carme Ruscalleda, moving from his native Argentina to Spain to do so. And one day he decided to settle in Ibiza.

Corrizos' passion and skill give Salvia its soul. He is a master of traditional and avant-garde techniques alike, of textures and flavors, and his skills are reflected in the menu's selection of typical tapas and dishes to share. Using local products and drawing inspiration from the Mediterranean, he creates creative, flawlessly executed dishes.

Potatoes are turned into poetic triple-cooked patatas bravas; carrots are marinated and roasted and served with yeast sauce, mirin, soy, and passion fruit puree. The grilled fennel, paired with stracciatella, beer mustard, and black garlic confit honey, is a story all its own. The vegetables come from the estate's own gardens. This zero-kilometer philosophy is important to the chef and guarantees the best quality.

Respect for this character! I'm already looking forward to the next time—it won't be long.

Far left – The zero-kilometer policy makes for top-quality ingredients.

Left – Head chef Pablo Carrizo is always driving the restaurant forward.

Below – In this picture-perfect setting, every meal is an experience.

GRILLED EGGPLANT WITH SOBRASADA

SERVES 2
DIFFICULTY

TOMATO JAM
1 kg ripe tomatoes (about 2 lb 3 oz)
300 g/10½ oz/1½ cups sugar
Salt

MISO SAUCE
1 tsp cornstarch
160 g/5½ oz dashi
150 g/5⅓ oz/generous ½ cup miso
200 ml/generous ¾ cup teriyaki sauce
100 ml/scant ½ cup sesame oil
100 ml/scant ½ cup sunflower oil

GRILLED EGGPLANT
1 eggplant
25 g/1 oz sobrasada
30 g/1½ oz feta
Chopped chives

1 For the tomato jam, cut or chop the tomatoes into pieces and place them in a saucepan with sugar, salt, and 100 ml/scant ½ cup water. Simmer on low heat for about 1 hour.

2 For the miso sauce, combine cornstarch and 200 ml/scant 1 cup water in a saucepan and heat gently, stirring, until thickened. Remove from heat and stir in the remaining ingredients.

3 Steam the eggplant in the oven for 20–30 minutes. Meanwhile, grill the sobrasada in the Josper oven or fry it in a pan, and crumble the feta with your fingers. Cut the eggplant in half and smoke it in a Josper oven, on the gas stove, or in a Big Green Egg.

4 Spread the miso sauce on the eggplant and top with the feta cheese. Arrange the sobrasada next to it and pipe some tomato jam on top using a piping bag. Serve sprinkled with chives.

THE GIRI CAFÉ

WITH HEART AND SOUL

W

THE GIRI CAFÉ
PLAZA ESPAÑA 5
07810 SAN JUAN
+34 971 333 474
giricafe.com

What a set of values! First: local or organic produce—the closer the better. Second: healthy, sophisticated dishes. Third: taste and texture are essential. Fourth: aesthetics—delicious food should look great, too. Fifth: guests deserve warm, friendly, and competent service.

Rosa Pil Hildebrandt is the owner and the heart and soul of the well-known Giri Café in San Juan, and the best example of how these strong values are lived out with passion. "We follow simple guidelines," she explains. "That means eating seasonally and buying local and sustainable—ideally at the market. We also have a garden. When we cook, we want to appeal to all the senses and prepare food with love. The greatest joy is celebrating a meal with others at a carefully set table."

You may not believe it, but you can taste and feel all of this when you visit the Giri Café. For the best—and most noticeable—experience, take a seat at one of the tables in the cozy garden. As soon as guests enter this oasis through the back door of the 300-year-old townhouse, the wafts of sweet and tart fragrance and abundance of colors compete with the food on the plates and in the bowls. As most of the ingredients are grown on site anyway, it becomes a harmonious overall culinary experience. Over 100 different plant species can be found in the outdoor area, including leafy vegetables, berries, herbs, and flowers. The garden not only provides ingredients, but also inspiration for future culinary creations. The other carefully selected ingredients come mainly from organic producers in Ibiza. "We have very good relationships with responsible suppliers on the island and the Spanish mainland," says Rosa.

Morning, noon, or night, any meal at the Giri Café is followed by an all-embracing feeling of wellbeing.

Left – Peaceful greenery: Surrounded by plants, everything tastes even better.

Below – At the tables out front, guests enjoy a fresh juice, smoothie, or drink.

Bottom – Director José Ramón Rodriguez, head chef Mayte Juárez Sánchez, sous chef Pilar Casquet Expósito.

ROASTED SWEET POTATO WITH GREEN TAHINI

SERVES 4
DIFFICULTY

PICKLED ONIONS
2 red onions
Juice of 2–3 lemons
Salt

ROASTED SWEET POTATOES
2 large sweet potatoes
Olive oil
Salt and pepper

GREEN TAHINI
½ bunch mint
½ bunch parsley
250 g/1 cup white tahini
Lemon juice
Salt

HERB OIL
½ bunch mint
½ bunch parsley
200 ml/scant 1 cup light olive oil

ROASTED CHERRY TOMATOES
200 g/7 oz red cherry tomatoes
Thyme
1 pinch of sugar
Salt

TO GARNISH
Roasted pumpkin seeds
Microgreens

1 For the pickled onions, start the day before. Peel the onions, cut into thin strips, and place in a jar. Lightly salt, cover with lemon juice, and chill.

2 For the roasted sweet potatoes, the next day preheat the oven to 200°C/400°F. Wash the sweet potatoes, pat dry and cut in half lengthwise. Drizzle the cut sides with olive oil and season with salt and pepper. Place on a sheet pan and bake for about 35 minutes until fully cooked. Set aside and turn the oven down to 120°C/250°F.

3 Meanwhile, for the green tahini, blend mint and parsley with olive oil in a blender until smooth. Add tahini and 2 ice cubes, blend again and season with lemon juice and salt. Keep chilled until serving.

4 For the herb oil, blanch mint and parsley for a few seconds in boiling water, then immediately cool in ice water. Pat dry with kitchen paper, blend with olive oil in a blender and set aside.

5 For the roasted cherry tomatoes, cut the tomatoes in half and place them on a baking tray. Sprinkle with thyme, sugar and salt, drizzle with olive oil and roast for 20 minutes at 120°C/250°F. Let them cool down.

6 Arrange the sweet potato halves on oval plates and top with green tahini, then the roasted cherry tomatoes and pickled onions. Garnish with roasted pumpkin seeds and microgreens, and drizzle with herb oil before serving.

SANT JOAN

1 EL SILENCIO

A popular beach club has put down roots in Cala Molí. The enchanting sister of the Paris nightclub of the same name, El Silencio exudes relaxed elegance. Argentine Mauro Colagreco (responsible for the Michelin stars of two restaurants on the Côte d'Azur) has run the kitchen since 2022 and is passionate about preparing the lunch and dinner menus on an open fire. The interior, with frequently changing art displays on the walls, is equally tasteful. Its inspiring flair comes from the creative minds from all walks of life, who list the restaurant on their vacation agenda. Mixologist Remy Savage brings special panache to the cocktail menu, capturing the very essence of joie de vivre in a glass for guests to consume. ***instagram.com/elsilencioibiza***

2 ES TORRENT

Nobody just stumbles on Es Torrent. The restaurant is located off the beaten track on the beach of the same name, and has to be sought out. The rewards for that persistence are white-clothed tables overlooking the ocean and set with platefuls of its bounty. The owners' values are deeply felt: "Gastronomy is our religion. The fishermen and farmers we trust are our allies. We practice zero-kilometer cuisine. Our raison d'être is to make our guests happy." What more could anyone want? Except, perhaps, to stretch out on one of the sun loungers after a meal and linger a little longer in the shade. ***estorrent.net/en/the-restaurant***

3 COTTON BEACH CLUB

A dream in white and the epitome of Ibiza's sparkling holiday vibes, the beach club in Cala Tarida attracts an exclusive clientele. Glamorous guests enjoy sushi with their signature rosé from Saint Tropez on the spacious terrace, gazing at the cloudless sky. Major island stars can be found in the DJ booth, setting the mood with the perfect music.
cottonlifestyle.com/cotton-beach-club-ibiza

4 SES BOQUES

6,000 pans of paella, 250 lemon cakes, 1,600 servings of salt-crusted fish: the impressive statistics from just one season at the beach restaurant in Es Cubells. By the way, the salt-crusted fish is on me—or rather, there's no way one woman can eat it alone, you'll need some hungry helpers—so, visit this laid-back family restaurant as a couple or, even better, with a group. On the rustic terrace, crowds of locals enjoy the freshly caught fish or equally fresh seafood. ***sesboques.com/en***

5 LOS ENAMORADOS

At the very top of Ibiza, practically where the island ends, in the village of Portinatx, an international couple has created Los Enamoradosa place for themselves and their guests to feel at home, sleep amid a boho atmosphere, eat "a little something," and shop for vintage design. ***losenamoradosibiza.com***

6 MON CHÂTEAU EN ESPAGNE

Bring along time to browse this treasure trove of pieces vintage and beyond. Located directly on the road to San Juan, it boasts a crammed display window. Inside, an Art Nouveau tea set rubs shoulders with a Murano glass menagerie, watched over by Hermès scarves, Cartier watches, and handbags from various elegant brands. ***instagram.com/monchateauenespagne.ibiza***

7 OBSOLETE

The gorgeous shop itself, right on the edge of San Juan, is already an inspiration—and so is its curated selection of furniture and decor. Dressers made from old wood, finds from Africa, linen-covered sofas, large ceramic pots, and lamps straight out of Wonderland. The walls usually display art (this time, it was striking black-and-white photos), which adds the finishing touch. ***instagram.com/obsolete_ibiza***

8 URUSUAI

A Tokyo-inspired tapas bar, Urusuai is ultra-cool and specializes in groundbreaking Iberian-Japanese fusion cuisine. It makes excellent use of the abundance of produce in the Balearic Islands and uses them in an way that captures their essence. The fine dining takes place in a breathtaking setting (think traditional Japanese tea room, bar with sea views, and elegant materials) and could easily lead to sensory overload if it weren't for the spectacular menu to provide a focus. Buttery-delicate chutoro tartare teamed with trout roe, wasabi cream, ponzu, and soy sauce; toro tamari sushi with caviar, wasabi, spring onions, and concentrated soy sauce; or aged wagyu cecina accompanied by pan con tomate shiso, which turns out to be milk bread and tomato paste of supreme quality (and a must-try), seasonal vegetable tempura with fermented garlic and honey, and hamachi carpaccio with trout roe and miso wasabi sauce. ***urusai-ibiza.com***

9 SIX SENSES

Good things come in threes, thinks the international luxury hotel chain Six Senses, which has opened its third European location on Ibiza. The resort at Cala Xarraca is set in a breathtaking landscape: the suites seem almost glued to the red cliffs, with the surf crashing below. From the high-ceilinged hall with huge windows, guests can start soaking up the beauty of the island's north at breakfast. The spa, with an array of massages, beauty treatments and therapies, is the ideal way to relax. The shop carries local products, with authentic goodies—olive oil, wine, salt, almonds, and more—that make perfect edible or drinkable souvenirs. The resort is run with attention and style, a place for memorable holiday experiences. ***sixsenses.com/en/hotels-resorts/europe/spain/ibiza***

SANTA EULARIA *des* RIU

PLAÇA
DE
LEPANT

A hotspot in the east.

SANTA EULÀRIA

des Riu

Beige sand, shallow water, and a well-kept promenade stretching along the sea and the river all come to mind when I think of Santa Eulària. Plus, the word "nice" fits perfectly, because the third largest town on Ibiza is extremely popular with families and children. The marina is more appealing to a mature crowd than the Marina Botafoch in Ibiza Town. The region's golf course and a few discreet, luxurious resort-style hotels also underline the atmosphere of respectability. A picture of the typical Santa Eulària fans starts to form.

The town provides a vibrant heart to the region of the same name, whose main artery is the only freshwater river in the entire Balearic Islands. The 18-kilometer (11-mile) Riu de Santa Eulària was once an essential water supply for the population, enabling fruit and vegetable cultivation and powering the mills for grain production. Even today, travelers can visit the Molí de Dalt o Can Planetes, a farmhouse with watermill, where a visitor center provides information about the river and its important role.

Those that can tear themselves away from their well-deserved holiday laziness for a brief bout of exertion will be richly rewarded—a walk up the hill near Santa Eulària leads to the simple, yet beautiful Puig de Missa church. The view inside and from the forecourt reveals the charm of the region. Incidentally, keep your eyes peeled at Eroski, the XL supermarket between the edge of town and the nearby beaches. You might just find yourself reaching for the same fruit as Campino, as the singer from Die Toten Hosen is a long-standing Ibiza resident. The beaches in this area are numerous, with the golden sands of Cala Llonga, Cala Nova and Cala Martina, and the lively buzz of Es Canar. At Aguas Blancas and Cala Mastella, the wind whips up the waves to create the perfect spot for surfers. Not to mention the other more or less secret coves just waiting to be discovered.

The promenade runs along the seafront and is lined with restaurants and bars.

There's plenty to discover here too.

The white architecture of Santa Eulària radiates Mediterranean tranquility.

AGUAMADERA

SILENCE IS A VIRTUE, STRESS IS AN ALIEN CONCEPT

AGUAMADERA
CTRA. DE JESÚS TO CALA LLONGA KM, 7.5
07819 SANTA EULALIA DES RIU
+34 623 994 411
aguamaderaibiza.com

It's so tempting to move straight in with bag and baggage. The no-frills finca brings peace to the souls of all who stay there. Tucked away on a hillside above Cala Llonga, Aguamadera Ibiza embodies a virtue that's so easy to lose. In the seven thoughtfully decorated rooms and four outbuildings of this agroturismo, individual creativity can awaken to life. The project was lovingly launched in 2023 by island artist (and daughter of the Pacha founder) Iria Urgell Calderón, and focuses on helping guests to reconnect with themselves.

As an ode to Ibiza's architectural past, the nineteenth-century building brings together terracotta tiles, whitewashed walls, and rustic wood surfaces in perfect harmony. Rough and soft textures are paired. The earthy color palette ties the whole seemingly effortless look together. Terraces, pools, an outdoor yoga platform, a wellness pavilion, and treatment rooms all help guests regain their inner balance. Workshops, retreats, and a host of treatments offer a wonderful way to relax.

The harmony and minimalist approach also extend to the already acclaimed cuisine of the in-house restaurant. It consistently upholds its heritage; chef Gonzalo Cerrato Laguna bases his craft and his work on the values of simplicity, purity, and sustainability, and has established a fire kitchen. The food is cooked over aromatic wood, giving a special smoky aroma to the produce that is harvested daily from the adjacent permaculture farm or sourced from selected local suppliers. Honest, authentic, and fiery.

Left – A place for contemplation, both indoors and outdoors.

Below – Executive Chef Gonzalo Cerrato Laguna oversees the estate's La Era restaurant.

Bottom – Agroturismo at its best.

ARTICHOKES WITH BÉARNAISE SAUCE AND SMOKED EEL

SERVES 6
DIFFICULTY

ARTICHOKES
5 artichokes
½ lemon
3 sprigs of parsley
1 clove of garlic
3 bay leaves
50 g/2 oz lemon thyme
Sunflower oil
Salt and pepper

SAUCE BÉARNAISE
100 g/4 oz shallots
100 ml/scant ½ cup white wine
100 ml/scant ½ cup white vinegar
10 peppercorns
2 egg yolks
200 g/8 oz clarified butter
5 g/1 tsp fresh tarragon
Salt

SMOKED EEL
Extra virgin olive oil
50 g/2 oz smoked eel

1 Prepare the artichokes: Remove the outer dark leaves, cut off the tips of the remaining leaves with a sharp knife, and peel the stem. Use a knife to carefully remove the fuzzy choke inside, taking care not to break the artichokes apart. Squeeze the lemon into a bowl of cold water and add the cleaned artichokes, the squeezed lemon, and the parsley.

2 Drain and place on a sheet pan with garlic, bay leaf, and thyme. Toss with sunflower oil, season with salt and pepper, and bake at 180°C/350°F for about 20 minutes.

3 For the béarnaise sauce, finely chop the shallots, place in a saucepan with white wine, vinegar, and peppercorns, and reduce over low heat until halved. Strain and cool. Whisk the egg yolks with the vinegar-wine reduction and a little salt, then place over a pot of boiling water. Turn off the heat and, whisking constantly, slowly add the melted butter in a thin stream. Remove from the heat as soon as the mixture combines and is creamy and thick. Finely chop the tarragon and add.

4 For the smoked eel, heat olive oil in a pan and quickly sear the eel. Remove and fry the artichokes in the remaining fat until golden brown.

5 Pour most of the béarnaise sauce onto a large plate, arrange the artichokes on top, and top with the smoked eel. Drizzle with the rest of the sauce, season with olive oil, salt, and pepper, and garnish with wild flowers if liked. Serve as hot as possible.

SEASONAL WILD MUSHROOMS

SERVES 2
DIFFICULTY

1 egg yolk
Soy sauce
150 g/5 oz porcini
150 g/5 oz níscalos (saffron milk caps)
150 g/5 oz black chanterelles
2 cloves of garlic
Olive oil
50 ml/scant ¼ cup white wine
100 ml/scant ½ cup chicken broth (optional)
1 bunch of parsley
Salt and pepper

1 Carefully place the egg yolk in a bowl and cover completely with soy sauce. Cover and let stand for a few hours.

2 Clean the mushrooms: Quarter the porcini and níscalos, leave the chanterelles whole, and slice the garlic thinly. Heat olive oil in a pan and fry the quartered mushrooms. Once they start to brown, add the chanterelles and garlic, and fry over high heat until the garlic begins to brown. Season with salt and pepper, deglaze with white wine, and allow to evaporate. Optionally, add chicken stock and reduce almost completely. Turn off the heat. Finely chop the parsley and stir in three-quarters of it.

3 Spread the mushrooms out on a large plate and make a well in the center. Lift the egg yolk out of the soy sauce with a slotted spoon, place it in the well, and serve sprinkled with the remaining parsley.

AMALUR

A GASTRONOMIC LANDMARK

AMALUR
CARRER SANT MIQUEL, KM. 2.3
07840 SANTA GERTRUDIS DE FRUITERA
+34 871 505 927
amalur.com

Anyone who succeeds in attracting gourmets to their island restaurant not just once, but repeatedly over a period of more than four decades simply has to be something special and have something to offer. Amalur can confidently be described as a culinary institution. It is a visual delight, with the pretty blue finca on the right-hand side of the road to Santa Gertrudis clearly showing that this is the home of style. The restaurant is named after the Basque goddess of Mother Earth, whose influences are reflected in the sophisticated dishes on the Italian-inspired and locally influenced menu.

Renowned restaurateur Francesco Manzoli brought Paolo Cortinovis into the restaurant as Executive Chef in July 2024. He is responsible for ensuring that the delicacies are created with such passion and prepared with such finesse. Guests can start with, say, a carpaccio of local tomatoes with arugula mayonnaise and basil, vitello tonnato, or melanzane alla Parmigiana. All sounds familiar and classic, but takes on a modern and extremely delicious twist. The next course is obligatory: homemade pasta, perhaps a sophisticated version of cacio y pepe or the popular pappardelle with pumpkin and Gorgonzola. The menu then takes to the water—offering sole with hazelnuts and citrus fruits, Formentera calamari in its own ink, and sea bass in a salt crust—or to land, with wafer-thin slices of warm beef or aged tenderloin with green pepper and potato millefeuille. Tiramisu would be a worthy finish, and if anyone finds a better one in Ibiza, please let me know.

Enough enthusiasm? No, because the presentation of the food is avant-garde and distinctive, the art on the walls is exquisite, the staff are ultra-friendly, and the decor only encourages guests to linger. Luckily, Amalur is open all year round, so we'll be booking again soon.

Far left – Guests are seated in the grand dining room, watched over by paintings.

Left – Paolo Cortinovis favors classic modern style in his cuisine.

Below – The blue finca has been attracting guests in droves for years.

PUMPKIN PAPPARDELLE WITH GORGONZOLA SAUCE

SERVES 4
DIFFICULTY

✹✹☼

FRESH PASTA
500 g/1 lb wheat flour
160 g/5½ oz egg yolk
30 ml/2 tbsp water

FILLING
Mantovana pumpkin (1.5 kg/3 lb)
350 g/12 oz grated Parmesan
8 amaretti
Salt and pepper

GORGONZOLA FONDUTA
1 kg/2 lb mild Gorgonzola
500 g/2 cups cream
500 ml/2 cups milk

FOR SERVING
Melted butter
Sage leaves
Amaretti
Roasted pumpkin seeds

1 Knead all the pasta ingredients into a smooth dough. Wrap in plastic wrap and set aside until ready to use.

2 For the filling, halve the pumpkin, place it in a baking dish, and bake at 150°C/300°F for 1 hour. Remove the skin and seeds, mash the flesh with a fork, and season with Parmesan, crumbled amaretti, salt, and pepper. Put the filling into a piping bag.

3 For the Gorgonzola fonduta, bring the milk and cream to a boil in a saucepan, stirring constantly. Remove from the heat, add the Gorgonzola (without the rind) and allow to melt. Pass the mixture through a fine sieve to remove any mold residue.

4 Using a pasta machine or rolling pin, roll out the pasta dough to extreme thinness and a length of 15 inches. Pipe the pumpkin filling down the middle of the dough and fold it over to enclose the filling. Cook the pappardelle in salted water for 3–4 minutes, scoop out, and drain. Toss with melted butter and sage.

5 Roll up the pappardelle strands into a rose shape, arrange on plates, and garnish with crumbled amaretti and toasted pumpkin seeds. Pour the Gorgonzola fonduta over the pappardelle and serve.

TOMATO CARPACCIO

SERVES 4
DIFFICULTY

TOMATO CARPACCIO
1 Barbastro pink tomato
1 blue tomato
1 Corazón de Buey tomato (oxheart)
Olive oil
Lime juice

PARSLEY BREADCRUMBS
200 g/8 oz breadcrumbs
150 g/5 oz fresh parsley
Salt

ROASTED TOMATO PASTE
1 Ibiza salad tomato
Parsley breadcrumbs
Olive oil

YELLOW CHERRY TOMATO CONFIT
6 yellow cherry tomatoes
Thyme
Lemon zest
Olive oil
Salt

ARUGULA MAYONNAISE
500 ml/2 cups olive oil
150 g/5 oz arugula
2 egg yolks
Salt

TO SERVE
Olive oil
Sherry vinegar
Toasted pine nuts
Basil
Salt

1 For the tomato carpaccio, slice the tomatoes into 2 thin slices each using a mandoline and drizzle with olive oil and lime juice.

2 For the parsley breadcrumbs, blend all the ingredients in a food processor into a green powder.

3 For the roasted tomato paste, halve the tomato and sprinkle with the parsley breadcrumbs. Place in an ovenproof dish and roast the tomatoes in a Josper oven or charcoal oven until cooked through. Remove the skin and seeds, mash the tomatoes, and drizzle with high-quality olive oil.

4 For the yellow cherry tomato confit, halve the tomatoes and season with thyme, lemon zest, olive oil, and salt. Place on a sheet pan and bake at 100°C/212°F for 1.5 hours.

5 For the arugula mayonnaise, place the olive oil and arugula in a Thermomix and blend for 1 minute on speed 10, then for 8 minutes on speed 6 (60°C/140°F). Strain through a cheesecloth. Whisk the egg yolks and arugula oil in a bowl until the thickness of mayonnaise, then season with salt and transfer to a piping bag.

6 Arrange the tomato slices for the carpaccio in a circle on a plate and season with sherry vinegar, olive oil, and salt. Top with the cherry tomato confit and add 6 teaspoons of roasted tomato paste. Pipe 8 small dots of arugula mayo onto the plate. Serve garnished with toasted pine nuts and basil.

Right – The restaurants to fall in love with, from New York to Ibiza.

Below – Lorenzo Seller cooks simple dishes with verve.

BOTTEGA IL BUCO

A NEW YORK INSTITUTION BRINGS ITALIANITÀ TO IBIZA

BOTTEGA IL BUCO
CARRER VÉNDA
DE PARADA, 12
07814 SANTA GERTRUDIS
DE FRUITERA
+34 971 197 676
ilbuco.com

At first glance, it is simply an inviting dining room with a glass-fronted bar through which guests can watch the two chefs (or an occasional chefess) bustling around and working their magic. On closer inspection, however, Bottega il Buco turns out to be a gem. The warmth is tangible as soon as you enter—even on your first visit. When il Buco co-founder Alberto Avalle is present, the welcome is a mix of "Hola!" and "Ciao." He and his partner Donna once founded the New York restaurants Alimentari and Vineria, creating legendary places for excellent, honest food, but also an exceptionally friendly atmosphere where guests can satisfy more than just their hunger. It's no coincidence that his establishments call themselves the "il Buco family."

The "family" philosophy is alive and well at the Ibiza outpost too. Only the best ingredients from both the region and Alberto's Italian homeland make the cut. A traditional focaccia *(see recipe)* is a staple at Bottega, with a variety of toppings that change with the seasons, so don't skip it. Best to go for a sampler of five different rectangular bites, topped with provolone and oregano, grilled zucchini, tomatoes… Everything else you order and eat is pretty much a "side dish." You might want to try one of the tins packed with sardines, mussels, or tuna. Burrata, paired with local strawberries, toasted hazelnuts, and green pistachio pesto *(see recipe)*, would be a perfect match. And since the roasted beetroot with oranges, chopped almonds, chili, and microgreens from the farm is as tasty as it is healthy, it really is worth a try. The aromatic salad with fresh herbs, fennel, pistachios, flowers, and citrus vinaigrette instantly became one of my favorites.

My first time at Bottega il Buco was some time ago. Since then, I've spent many more lunches and dinners at one of those wooden tables, eating something delicious from the beautiful, handmade ceramic dishes and recharging my batteries. But save a little room for dessert—the tiramisu. It's perfect for sharing, too.

FOCACCIA

SERVES 4
DIFFICULTY

500 g/1 lb flour
150 g/5 oz sourdough starter
3 g/½ tsp yeast
10 g/2 tsp fine sea salt
5 g/1 tsp granulated sugar
5 tbsp extra virgin olive oil and more for spreading
¼ tsp coarse sea salt
1 sprig rosemary, needles plucked

1 In the bowl of a stand mixer, combine flour, sourdough starter, yeast, and 375 ml/generous 1½ cup warm water. Knead with the dough hook on low speed for about 5 minutes, then increase to medium speed and knead for another 5 minutes until the dough starts to look shiny and pulls away from the hook. Cover the bowl with a towel and let it rest at room temperature for 20 minutes.

2 Meanwhile, mix the fine sea salt and sugar in a small bowl. After the resting time, sprinkle the mixture over the dough and work in until no grains remain.

3 Brush a sheet pan with 2 tablespoons of olive oil. Coat the dough with oil, too, and place it on the pan. Cover with plastic wrap and let rest overnight in the fridge.

4 The next day, preheat the oven to 230°C/450°F top/bottom heat and let the dough come to room temperature. Drizzle 1 tablespoon of olive oil over the dough, gently press small dimples into the surface with your fingers, and flatten slightly without tearing. Sprinkle with the remaining olive oil, coarse salt, and rosemary needles.

5 Bake the focaccia on the middle rack of the preheated oven for 15 minutes, rotate the pan through 180 degrees, and bake for another 15 minutes until golden brown. Cool on a rack and serve with the finest olive oil.

BURRATA WITH STRAWBERRIES

SERVES 1–2
DIFFICULTY
✹ ☼ ☼

BASIL OIL
1 bunch basil
150 ml/generous ½ cup sunflower oil

VINAIGRETTE
50 g/2 oz honey
70 g/⅓ cup vinegar
400 ml/scant 1¾ cups extra virgin olive oil
Sea salt

TO SERVE
7 strawberries (or 1 nectarine)
1 handful pink tomatoes
1 handful datterini tomatoes
1 ball of burrata
Sea salt

1 For the basil oil, pick the basil leaves and set a few aside for garnish. Blanch the rest in boiling water for 30 seconds, drain, and immediately chill in ice water. Drain well, then blend with sunflower oil in a blender until smooth. Strain through a cloth, pour into a squeeze bottle, and set aside.

2 Whisk together the ingredients for the vinaigrette.

3 Quarter the strawberries, or slice the nectarine into wedges instead. Halve the datterini tomatoes, toss them with the vinaigrette in a bowl, and let them sit for a bit. Slice the pink tomatoes thinly and arrange them overlapping on a plate. Gently pull apart the burrata with your fingers and place it on top. Spoon the marinated datterini tomatoes over, and arrange the strawberries or nectarines around. Drizzle with basil oil, season with salt, and serve garnished with basil leaves.

NAGAI

LONG LIVE INDULGENCE

NAGAI
CARRETERA A
SANT JOAN, 5, KM. 9
07840 SANTA EULÀRIA
+34 689 675 825
nagairestaurant.com

W

Wow, there's so much. And so much variety! The menu at Nagai is so extensive that ordering may take a while—unless you're one of the many regulars who can rattle off their favorite dishes without even glancing at the menu. Everyone else takes their time reading it, preferably with a drink in hand.

But goodness, the drinks menu seems just as endless. In addition to various sakes and wines, including sparkling options, you could have a Bloody Nagai or a Nippon Cosmopolitan from the Classics menu, a Purple Rain from the Signatures, or—to keep a clear head when choosing your meal—a Fruit Loop from the Virgins. And here we go: You're likely to lose track as you try to assemble a reasonable order from the ranges of hot tapas, raw dishes, salads, tempuras, stir-fries, and meat and fish specialties. To make matters worse, some dishes are marked with a star. This designates the *sabor d'Eivissa*, the taste of Ibiza, and highlights the fact that choosing the marked dish supports local farmers and fishermen.

Back to being reasonable—probably not a vital consideration at Nagai—but first-timers have it easiest if they just order the tempting Chef's Selection, a sushi and sashimi platter. Artfully arranged nigiri (including tuna belly and eel), sashimi of sea bass or wild salmon, dragon or scallop rolls, and more Japanese treats will soon be brought to your table by smiling staff. While you wait, you can browse the little boutique in the back of the restaurant for the Nagai clothing line and other cool finds.

The atmosphere at the evening restaurant is always lively, the lighting muted, the walls painted dark. The music comes from live performances or the DJ booth and is sometimes a few decibels too loud, so it's better to gaze yearningly at your companion in silence. Fortunately, there is plenty to watch in the restaurant, where the one and only Reina rules over the kitchen. She is the queen of the quartet of owners, alongside Eleonora (head of good ideas), Melchior (convincing communicator), and Luigi (go-to for everything).

The name Nagai says it all: It's the Japanese word for longevity. See for yourself how long an evening there will linger in the memory.

Far left – The place is a beacon from afar.

Left – The decor has an Asian touch.

Below – Reina adds finesse to the culinary delights.

SCALLOP CARPACCIO

SERVES 1
DIFFICULTY

3 scallops (sashimi quality)
80 g/3 oz leek
50 g/2 oz edamame (shelled)
Piece of kombu, about 3 cm x 3 cm/ 1.2 in x 1.2 in (dried seaweed, kelp)
¼ avocado
10 ml/2 tsp olive oil
5 ml/1 tsp lemon juice
Salt, 1 g/pinch of sansho pepper

TRUFFLE VINAIGRETTE
3 slices black summer truffle
15 ml/1 tbsp olive oil
15 ml/1 tbsp lemon juice
5 tbsp agave syrup
1 pinch kombu powder (optional)
Salt

GARNISH
Edible flowers (optional)
Chopped chives

1 For the carpaccio, slice 2½ scallops into thin, even slices. Cut the remaining half-scallop into 5 mm/0.2 inch cubes and set aside.

2 For the avocado purée, finely chop the leek. Cook 30 g/1 oz leek with edamame and kombu in 100 ml/scant ½ cup of lightly salted water for 10 minutes over medium heat. Remove from heat, strain through a sieve and save the liquid; remove the kombu. Blend a third of the liquid with the cooked leek, edamame, avocado, olive oil, lemon juice, and sansho pepper in a mini blender or milk frother until smooth.

3 Cook the remaining 50 g/2 oz leek in the remaining cooking liquid until soft; drain and salt. Use a kitchen blowtorch to toast it until almost charred. Salt the scallop cubes and torch them until golden brown.

4 For the truffle vinaigrette, finely chop the truffles, mix with the other ingredients, and season to taste.

5 Place a 6–7 cm/2.4-2.8 inch aluminum ring on a plate and pour in the purée. Top with the scallop slices and carefully remove the ring. Arrange the charred leek and scallop cubes around, and sprinkle with edible flowers and chives if desired. Drizzle with truffle vinaigrette and serve.

SOBA NOODLES WITH TUNA AND RED SHRIMP

SERVES 1
DIFFICULTY
✹✹☼

DASHI SAUCE
Piece of kombu about 3 cm x 3 cm/ 1.2 in x 1.2 in (dried seaweed, kelp)
10 g/2 tsp katsuobushi (bonito flakes)
10 g/2 tsp sugar
20 ml/4 tsp soy sauce

TARTARE
50 g/2 oz red tuna fillet (sashimi quality)
3 red shrimp
1 umeboshi (Japanese salted plum)
10 g/2 tsp yuzu miso (miso with yuzu zest and juice; or white miso with grated lime zest)
5 ml/1 tsp agave syrup
30 g/generous 1 oz ikura (salmon roe)
Salt

SOBA
80 g/3 oz soba (buckwheat noodles)

GARNISH
20 g/1 oz chopped spring onions
½ tsp sesame
1 shiso leaf, finely sliced
Wasabi (optional)

1 For the dashi sauce, soak kombu in 100 ml/ scant ½ cup of water for 15 minutes, then add the katsuobushi and bring to a boil. Simmer for 5 minutes, then strain through a sieve. Remove the bonito flakes, return the kombu to the liquid, and simmer with sugar and soy sauce for another 5 minutes on low heat. Remove the kombu and chill the sauce until ready to use.

2 For the tartare, cut the tuna into 5 mm/0.2-inch cubes. Remove the head, shell, and gut from the shrimp, and cut the meat into the same size cubes too. Pit the umeboshi and crush into a smooth paste with a knife.

3 Gently mix the tuna and shrimp cubes with the umeboshi paste, yuzu miso, and agave syrup. Season with salt and carefully fold in the ikura, making sure not to crush the eggs.

4 For the noodles, cook the soba in plenty of water according to the package instructions, drain, and rinse under cold running water. Chill in ice water for 2 minutes, then drain thoroughly.

5 Arrange the chilled soba noodles in a deep plate and pour the cold dashi sauce over them. Sprinkle with spring onions, sesame, and shiso strips, and serve the tartare in a separate small bowl on the side.

6 Mix the soba noodles with the tartare at the table and season with wasabi to taste.

OVERALL

A LIBRARY OF FLAVORS

W

OVERALL
PASSEIG DE SANTA GERTRUDIS N11, LOCAL 3
07814 SANTA GERTRUDIS DE FRUITERA
+34 683 399 023
overallibiza.com

What happens when two inquisitive talents immerse themselves in the study of flavors, aroma extraction, and preservation methods? The results look pretty awesome, and taste even better. Overall in Santa Gertrudis is hard to capture in words—but that seems to be exactly what owners Mónica A. Patiño Primera and Jorge A. Conde want. That's why, instead of an "About" page, their website has a button asking "wtf is Overall" that provides no more than a tantalizing scrap of information.

But this is only the starting point. The Flavour Atelier—as the duo calls their 2021-founded restaurant—creates tailor-made experiences time after time. A magical synergy reigns between kitchen and bar; both are inspired by Ibiza and the changing seasons, and use the same ingredients for both food and drinks. So you can even eat a Bloody Mary here. The ambitious couple loves to research and experiment, and are masters of both traditional and modern techniques: "We see it as our duty to develop ideas using the knowledge we have gained from over 15 years of experience. Our goal is to create a library of flavors in our pantry," they explain. "We get bored quickly, so our menus are based on innovation, always frequently evolving and changing—sometimes even within a single week."

The couple even devised a special design for the dining area: two open workspaces set up as a "chef's table," a long, comfortable counter seating up to 24 guests per session, and minimalist decor with an underground feel, avant-garde graffiti on the walls, and dramatic lighting.

This concept restaurant serves elaborate omakase menus. The "Basic" is a 4- to 5-course dinner created by the chef using seasonal market finds, small-batch quality ingredients, and specialties from their flavor library. Or go for the "Pro" with 5 to 6 courses. Then there's the "Omakase Expert," where gourmets can taste their way through 7 to 9 courses. Drink pairings are basically a must, perfectly matching the unusual drinks (alcoholic, low-alcohol, or non-alcoholic) to your chosen experience.

After more than 15 years in the restaurant world, with stops in Spain, England, and Singapore, Jorge and Mónica have now settled down and started a family in Ibiza. *Bona sort*!

Left – In the restaurant with bar, everything is flawlessly coordinated.

Below – Co-owner Mónica is in her element.

TRUFFLE TARTLET

SERVES 2
DIFFICULTY

✹✹✹

COCOA TARTLET
225 g/8 oz wheat flour
20 g/1 oz unsweetened cocoa powder
50 g/2 oz powdered sugar or icing sugar
120 g/4 oz very cold unsalted butter
1 egg
Fine salt

TARTARE
300 g/10 oz smoked venison ham
(or game ham or beef ham)
1 tsp sriracha sauce
1 tsp pickle brine
1 tsp smoked maple seasoning (optional)
1 tsp herb oil
1 tsp coarse sweet mustard
1 bunch chives
1 red onion
1 seasonal truffle
Sea salt and black pepper

1 For the tartlet, sift flour, cocoa powder, powdered sugar, and a pinch of salt into the bowl of a food processor. Add the cubed butter and pulse to a fine, crumbly texture. Add the beaten egg and pulse again to form a sticky dough.

2 Shape the dough into a disk and roll out between two sheets of baking paper to a circle about 3 mm/0.1 inch thick. Chill for at least 1 hour or up to 24 hours, then remove the paper, cut small circles from the dough, and gently press them into the wells of a muffin tin. Press the edge between the bottom and sides lightly to get rid of air bubbles, and prick the bottom with a fork. Chill for at least 1 hour or up to 24 hours.

3 Preheat the oven to 160°C/320°F top/bottom heat. Meanwhile, put the muffin tins in the freezer.

4 Line the dough wells with baking paper and fill with baking beads, dried beans, or rice. Blind bake for 15 minutes, then remove the weights and paper and bake for another 15 minutes. Cool completely before removing from the molds.

5 Meanwhile, prepare the tartare: Finely chop the meat with a knife and mix with sriracha sauce, pickle brine, maple spice (optional), herb oil, and mustard. Slice the chives into thin rings, finely chop the onion, and mix both into the tartare. Season with salt and pepper. Fill the tart shells with the tartare and serve topped generously with freshly shaved truffle.

6 We serve this savory dessert as one of the final courses of an omakase experience.

RAW WILD-CAUGHT FISH WITH SOUR APPLE

SERVES 2
DIFFICULTY
✹✹✹

SOUR APPLE PRESERVES
1 apple (Granny Smith)
2 tbsp powdered sugar
½ tsp grated ginger
½ tsp citric acid

QUICK KOHLRABI PICKLE
1 kohlrabi
100 ml/scant ½ cup white soy sauce
50 ml/scant ¼ cup sake
½ tsp grated ginger
Herbs

TO SERVE
1 wild-caught white fish fillet
Dried kombu (seaweed)
2 tbsp extra virgin olive oil with herbs
1 tbsp soy sauce
Various herbs, e.g., tarragon, dill, parsley, cilantro
Grated ginger
Salt

1 For the quick sour apple pickle, slice the apple very thinly. Mix powdered sugar with 1 tbsp water, ginger, and citric acid, and pour over the apple slices to cover. Chill for at least 24 hours.

2 For the quick kohlrabi pickle, peel and very finely slice the kohlrabi and mix with white soy sauce, sake, ginger, and herbs as desired. Place in a screw-top jar and chill for 3 days. For a longer version, mix the kohlrabi with white soy sauce, sake lees, ginger, and herbs, place in a sterilized jar, and mature in the refrigerator for about 3 months.

3 For Overall's fish crudo, the whole fish is usually dried for about 6 days; however, for home use, it's easier to wrap the fish fillet in kombu and dry in the fridge for 3–4 hours. This boosts the flavor and makes the texture much easier to handle.

4 Take the fish out of the fridge and remove the kombu. Slice the fillet into 3–4 mm/about ⅛ inch thick pieces and marinate in a bowl with herb oil, soy sauce, and sea salt. Leave to stand briefly.

5 Arrange the apple slices on a plate, top with the fish slices, and garnish with a few slices of kohlrabi. Sprinkle with freshly grated ginger and chopped herbs before serving.

6 The fish crudo is perfect as a starter for a tasting menu or as a palate-cleanser between courses.

SANTA G. BAGEL HOUSE

OMG

SANTA G. BAGEL HOUSE
PASSEIG DE SANTA GERTRUDIS N11, LOCAL 3
07814 SANTA GERTRUDIS DE FRUITERA
+34 683 399 023
overallibiza.com/bagelhouse

A

A good day starts with a black coffee and a rainbow bagel—at least if you ask Jorge Conde, Mónica Patiño, and their growing fanbase. This foodie couple have opened a fantastic daytime café in Santa Gertrudis, all about artisan bagels & speciality coffee. The stylishly tiled Santa G. Bagel House even has a terrace overlooking the village church. The chefs pour their passion, precision, and creativity into every single bagel. Call it punctilious, call it meticulous, but it really is possible to taste the difference. To learn something or discover the secrets behind their creations, just watch the crew as they hand-roll and bake the dough while they chop, sizzle, stir, and portion out the toppings.

It seems that nobody rests until everything is perfect. The result is a plateful of top-notch craftsmanship and a real treat for the tastebuds. The team loves to experiment with flavors and textures, so first-timers might have a hard time choosing. The combo of house-smoked salmon on local goat cheese and refreshing cucumber in an open seeded bagel is intriguing, but the salty trout roe with aromatic herbs, seaweed, and chives sounds just as exciting. Smoked pastrami with marinated vegetables is a fresh take on a New York classic. Vegetarians can go for a pretzel bagel with mushrooms, cherry tomatoes, peppers, and zucchini. Play it safe with the Clásico with salmon, cream cheese, tomatoes, and capers—always a winner. Or go hearty with a rainbow bagel loaded with cheddar, fried egg, and bacon.

As an accompaniment, hand-brewed filter coffee is available hot or as cold-brew. But wait, this is not just any coffee! The sparkling cold-brew coffee with hibiscus is quite the revelation. All coffees are made with beans from small suppliers and ground just before brewing. Precision and dedication make all the difference, even with "simple" things like bagels and coffee.

Far left – Coffee as an art form, perfected here.

Left – Jorge and Mónica live and work together.

Below – Cool spot for a quick treat.

KYOTO CUCUMBER ON EVERYTHING BAGEL

SERVES 1
DIFFICULTY
✹✹✹

SEA WATER CUCUMBER
1 cucumber
Ibiza y Formentera Agua de Mar (filtered hypertonic sea water with high mineral content; or water with 3.5–3.8% sea salt)
2 tbsp vinegar
½ bunch dill (optional)
1 tsp roasted sesame, coriander, or cumin (optional)

SOY CUCUMBERS
1 cucumber
50 ml/scant ¼ cup high-quality soy sauce
20 ml/4 tsp mirin or sake (optional)
½ tsp wasabi, horseradish, or ginger (optional)

TO SERVE
1 "everything bagel" (e.g. with poppy seeds, sunflower seeds, white and black sesame)
Salted butter
¼ cucumber
Wasabi furikake (Japanese spice mix with sesame and dried seaweed; Asian store)
Salt and pepper

1 For the fermented seawater cucumbers, slice the cucumber into about 3 mm/0.1 inch slices using a mandoline and soak in hypertonic seawater and vinegar of your choice. Optionally, add dill and toasted sesame, coriander, or cumin. Place in a vacuum bag, seal, and chill for a few days.

2 For the soy cucumbers, slice the cucumber into about 7 mm/¼ inch slices and soak in soy sauce, adding sake or mirin if desired. For a little heat, add grated wasabi, horseradish, or ginger. Seal in a vacuum bag and chill for a few days.

3 To serve, quickly heat or toast the bagel in the oven, slice horizontally, and spread both halves with butter. Thinly slice the cucumber, season with salt and pepper, and layer it on the bagel, then add about half the seawater cucumbers, and finally about a quarter of the soy cucumbers. Sprinkle with furikake and serve.

4 The fresh combination of salted butter, cucumbers, and wasabi also works brilliantly on toasted sourdough bread or rice.

SMOKED BLACK ANGUS BRISKET ON RAINBOW BAGEL

SERVES 2
DIFFICULTY
✸✸✸

SMOKED BLACK ANGUS BRISKET
6 kg/12 pound joint of marbled Black Angus brisket
Oil
Coarsely ground mustard seeds
Coarsely ground black pepper
Coarsely ground spices as desired, e.g., allspice, Asian chilies, coriander seeds, paprika, garlic or onion powder
Salt

SLAW
350 g/12 oz red cabbage
1 red onion
20 ml/4 tsp Japanese mayonnaise
Olive oil
Salt and pepper

GLAZE
Maple syrup
Mustard seeds
Brandy

TO SERVE
2 rainbow bagels (or regular bagels or toasted sourdough)

1 For the smoked brisket, take the meat, which preferably has good muscle and a good layer of fat, brush with oil, and rub generously with spices. Heat the smoker to 75°C/170°F and fill with a mixture of oak, apple, and hickory wood. Smoke the meat for about 30 hours or until it reaches an internal temperature of 74°C/about 165°F—the exact time depends on the size. Then wrap the meat tightly in foil and steam in the oven at 130°C/250°F for about 2 hours. Rest at room temperature for at least 1 hour before slicing. Cut into slices as thin or thick as you like. If you can't smoke it yourself, buy smoked meat from the butcher and sear it at home.

2 For the slaw, use a mandoline to slice the red cabbage and onion very thinly and mix with mayo and olive oil in a bowl. Season with salt and pepper and let stand for a while.

3 For the glaze, bring maple syrup, pickled mustard seeds, and brandy to a boil and reduce slightly.

4 To serve, briefly heat or toast the bagels in the oven and slice horizontally. Place the slaw on the bottom half, top with the brisket, and brush with glaze. Put the top half on, wrap in paper, and cut in half with a sharp knife.

OLEOTECA SES ESCOLES

100 PERCENT EXTRA VIRGIN

OLEOTECA SES ESCOLES
CARRETERA SANT JOAN, KM. 9
07840 SANTA GERTRUDIS
+34 871 870 229
sesescoles.com

Would you willingly go back to school? I'm pretty sure you would if it was Ses Escoles—although the hard benches of the old schoolhouse have been replaced by comfy chairs and the purpose is now totally different. Once a place of learning, the school now focuses on the art of cooking.

The heart and soul of the market kitchen at Ses Escoles is oil—and specifically, olive oil from the restaurant's own mill, Gan Miquel Guasch. There are delicious ways to use mild, sweet Arbequina, intense, slightly bitter Picual, or a blend of both; they're drizzled over thin, crisp bread with fresh tomatoes, or used to liven up vegetables with Spanish romesco sauce. Wild green asparagus, fried in this oil and served with parmesan zabaglione, is also delicious.

In fact, the entire kitchen team is passionate about Ibizan tradition. The hearty farmer's salad made with roasted peppers is a classic at the end of summer on Ibiza, when the peppers in the gardens glow bright red until the rain ends the season. It's served as a starter or as a side with grilled meat or sardines.

Most dishes come straight from the impressive grill to your plate. From the big dining room, you can peek into the kitchen, where the grill is the star. The charcoal gives everything a signature smoky flavor that takes skill to master, but the turbot with fried garlic is always cooked perfectly—just like the lamb chops.

The place is also a visual treat. From the outside, its stone façade and bright doors on the road from Ibiza Town to San Juan are a landmark that seems to confirm to guests: You're on the right track.

Left – Housed in a former school, the restaurant now teaches matters of the palate.

Below – Simple but top-notch ingredients usually end up on the grill.

Bottom – The whole team is dedicated to hospitality.

COCA DE ESCALIVADA

A TRADITIONAL CATALAN DISH

SERVES 4
DIFFICULTY
✹✹✹

500 g/1 lb wheat flour
30 g/1 generous ounce fresh yeast
65 ml/generous ¼ cup extra virgin olive oil. plus extra for baking and serving
1 blanched bell pepper
1 blanched eggplant
Anchovies in oil
1 tsp salt

1 Mix flour, yeast, and 200 ml/scant 1 cup water in a bowl and knead into a compact dough. Cover with a cloth and leave to rise at room temp for 3 hours. Knead again, work in the olive oil, cover, and leave to rest for another 30 minutes.

2 Flatten and roll out the dough with a rolling pin. Oil a sheet pan and lay the dough on it. Slice the vegetables—the escalivada—into strips and spread them on top. Bake at 180°C/350°F for about 20 minutes.

3 Top the coca de escalivada with anchovies and serve drizzled with olive oil.

FARMER'S SALAD

SERVES 2
DIFFICULTY

4 red bell peppers
½ bulb of garlic
4 large potatoes
1 onion
Extra virgin olive oil
Salt

1 Grill the peppers in the oven, in a grill pan, or preferably over charcoal until soft, turning occasionally. Grill the halved garlic bulb for about 5 minutes. Let both cool slightly, then remove the burnt skin and seeds. Slice the peppers into strips, and peel and finely chop the garlic.

2 Boil or microwave the potatoes in boiling water for about 14 minutes, depending on size. Peel and chop them.

3 Slice the onion into six wedges and grill for a few minutes until done, then slice into strips.

4 Mix everything together in a salad bowl and season with olive oil and salt. The salad is traditionally served warm but can be enjoyed at room temperature, too.

BIO

WILD BEETS

FROM AVOCADO TO ONION

WILD BEETS
CARRETER VENDA DE CAN LLÀTZER, 9
07814 SANTA GERTRUDIS DE FRUITERA
+34 971 197 870
wildbeets.com

T

The simple restaurant with the eye-catching sign at the entrance to Santa Gertrudis proclaims to be no less than the future of food. And according to Wild Beets, that means raw, vegetarian or vegan, gluten-free, and more. The main ingredient? Thinking outside the box: no labels, no rules, no dogmas. Practicing this philosophy, Wild Beets has spent years feeding people who want to treat their bodies right. "Every dish on our menu is carefully crafted to pack in the maximum nutrients and the maximum flavor. By combining science with cooking skills and a passion for plant-based foods, we raise awareness of good food in every sense," says chef Cliff Grubin.

For breakfast, the spinach "n'omelet" has been a hit since day one and has been further perfected over the years. Kimchi roesti and açai bowls with chia seeds or granola are also extremely popular. At lunch, the raw coconut pad thai is the bestseller: "The pad thai with raw coconut is one of the stars of our new lunch menu. It's an incredibly tasty dish—colorful, fresh, and full of fun textures and flavors," says Cliff Grubin. When he was still a tireless traveler, Ibiza inspired him to make a stopover—and he's still there. All the island's mindful gourmets hope he'll stay around for a long, long time.

Far left – An unmissable location at the entrance to the village.

Left – Gaston Stivelmaher is utterly convinced by what he does.

Below – The little front garden is a haven for diners.

CHICKPEA OMELET

SERVES 6
DIFFICULTY
✹✹☼

CASHEW CREAM CHEESE
350 g/13 oz cashew nuts
10 ml/2 tsp olive oil
2 probiotic capsules
5 g/1 tsp salt

FILLING
Extra virgin olive oil
2 kg/4 lb leaf spinach
Pinch of nutmeg
Salt and pepper

OMELET
200 g/8 oz chickpea flour
75 ml/generous ¼ cup extra virgin olive oil plus more for frying
350 ml/1½ cups water
1 tsp garlic powder
1 tsp turmeric
1 tsp black salt
Pepper

TO SERVE
3 tomatoes, halved and baked or fried in a very hot pan until golden
300 g/10 oz fried mushrooms
Chopped chives or other herbs

1 For the cashew cream cheese, start the day before by soaking the cashews in water and chilling them for at least 12 hours. Drain and rinse the nuts until the water runs clear. Place the nuts in a food processor with 150 ml/generous ½ cup fresh water, olive oil, the contents of the probiotic capsules, and salt, and blend until smooth. Keep chilled.

2 Heat olive oil in a pan and wilt the spinach. Season with nutmeg, salt, and pepper. If the spinach does not fit in the pan, repeat the process if necessary until all the spinach is cooked. Cool, chop, and mix with the cashew cream cheese.

3 Meanwhile, blend all the ingredients for the omelet until smooth and chill for 1 hour.

4 Heat olive oil in a pan. Cover the bottom with one-sixth of the omelet mixture and fry for about 2 minutes until set. Carefully lift out or slide onto a plate. Make 6 omelets in this way.

5 Spread the cashew-spinach mix on the omelets and fold into half-moons. Serve the omelets with roasted tomatoes, mushrooms, and chives.

PAD THAI WITH COCONUT

SERVES 6
DIFFICULTY

2 carrots
Peel of 1 cucumber
200 g/8 oz cabbage
1 red onion
1 red bell pepper
4 young coconuts
200 g/8 oz sprouts
Salt

SAUCE
300 g/10 oz tamarind paste
40 ml/8 tsp agave syrup
40 ml/8 tsp lime juice
30 ml/6 tsp tamari (or soy sauce)
1 jalapeño or habanero pepper
20 g/1 oz ginger
15 g/¾ oz garlic
40 g/1½ oz peanut butter
Water from 4 coconuts

TO SERVE
Lime wedges
Chopped peanuts
Chives

1 Slice carrots, cucumber peel, cabbage, onion, and peppers into thin strips. Halve the coconuts, saving the coconut water for the sauce, and scoop out the flesh, slicing it as finely as possible.

2 Blend all the ingredients for the sauce in a blender until smooth.

3 Mix the vegetable strips, coconut flesh, and sprouts in a bowl with the sauce and season with salt to taste.

4 Arrange on plates and serve garnished with lime wedges, chopped peanuts, and a few chives.

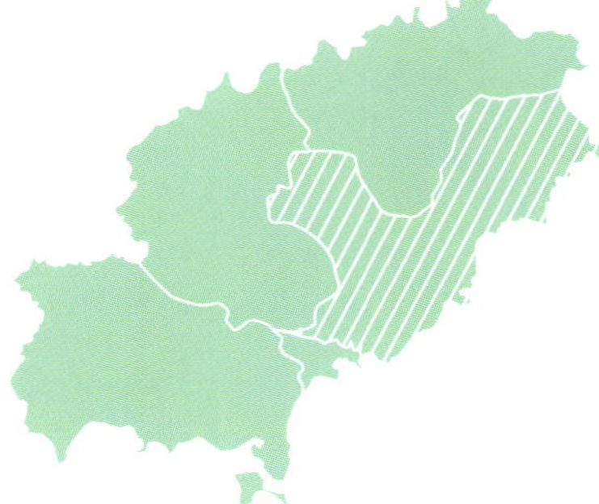

SANTA EULÀRIA

1 GATZARA SUITES

The staff at this family-run boutique hotel in Santa Gertrudis welcomes guests in the tall entrance hall, off which bright rooms with decor of light wood, natural stone tiles, marble, and plenty beige and white lead. A host of services—from babysitting to spa and gym—plus activities like bike tours are all part of the package. Take a stroll through the village to the "holy" Pou d'en Gatzara well that gave the hotel its name. ***hotelgatzaraibiza.com***

3 MEKE

Ibiza's ultimate coffee is served at Meke's own café in Santa Eulalia and at the San Juan market, where it feels like the whole island gathers. But the roastery is also worth a visit to talk shop about barista skills, sample the best oat milk for a perfect cappuccino, and pick up the ideal ACME cup. ***meke.coffee***

2 LA GALERIA ELEFANTE

Want to bring home a little something from Ibiza? This colorfully curated store in Santa Gertrudis brings together delightful souvenirs under one roof: silk or batik dresses, embroidered pillows, rugs, notebooks, sparkly postcards, crystal jewelry, a men's collection, and plenty of adorable knick-knacks. The owner supports local artisans with her selection. ***lagaleriaelefante.com***

4 PARADA

In the heart of the village of Santa Gertrudis stands a distinctive white finca with blue paint. Inside, shopkeepers display carefully selected treasures, from ceramics to clothing and cosmetics to children's items. You're sure to pick up one or two, or three, pretty things to take home.
instagram.com/parada.ibiza

5 NUMERO 74

You'll find handmade clothes for you and your mini-me at this atelier-style shop in Santa Gertrudis and on Formentera. The collections are super inspiring, and you can dive into them with creative workshops.
numero74.com

6 KSAR LIVING

Alberto, the owner of the large furniture store on the road through the island, has a keen eye for interior design. He loves combining wooden tables, rugs, seating elements, and console tables from Morocco, Bali, and Spain and dressing them with art and tableware. Chatting with this style expert is always a treat.
ksarliving.com

7 SIEMPRE

On Ibiza, decorating is a way of life. The store in Santa Gertrudis focuses on stylish homewares in muted colors with a touch of ethnic chic. Lamps, mirrors, scented candles (with coordinating matches!), dishes, cutlery, and horn bowls are all beautifully displayed and ready to inspire you. ***instagram.com/siempre_deco_ibiza***

8 MACAO CAFÉ

The restaurant with its tree-shaded terrace in Santa Gertrudis has been attracting a classy (and kind of cult) crowd for years. The Italian food is classic—at worst solid, at best outstanding. If you weren't in the mood before, the lively vibe will get you there. By the end, you'll be saying: What an awesome night. ***instagram.com/macaocafesanta gertrudis***

CHEZ BIBI 9

"Baked happiness" could be the motto of this sweet spot in Santa Gertrudis. People from all over the island flock to the bakery café to stock up on focaccia, olive bread, and all sorts of treats: the cinnamon rolls are usually sold out by noon, but the crumb cakes, lemon-poppy seed cake, berry tarts, and pains aux raisins are just as good. If you want to hang out in Santa Gertrudis for a while, grab a seat inside by the big bakery or outside on the terrace in the shade of an umbrella, and order a sweet treat with a reviving coffee or punchy ginger tea. Who needs anything more.
instagram.com/chez_bibi_von_bakery_ibiza

FORMEN-
TERA

FORMEN-TERA

Ibiza's little sister is full of lovely spots.

The lighthouse is a magnet for visitors and a landmark in Formentera.

An islet as if deposited by divine hands: Formentera, Ibiza's little sister, charms visitors who appreciate unspoiled beauty. As the smallest and southernmost of the Balearic Islands, it has retained its character and endearing unconventionality despite the growing flocks of tourists.

Many come for a day trip, but this picturesque destination is best explored slowly, so that a stay of several days is definitely worthwhile. New arrivals take the ferry from Ibiza's port to the former fishing village of La Savina, a 30- to 45-minute journey. From there, the pace slows a little—and that's a good thing. It's a good idea to rent a bike or scooter and continue at a leisurely pace. Covering a total of 83 square kilometers (32 square miles), Formentera has plenty to offer, with extensive white sandy beaches, dunes providing shelter from the scorching July sun, pale blue waters, and, of course, numerous beach bars, some still with a charming rustic feel and serving authentic Mediterranean food.

Formentera also seems to have something special: a creative energy. Joni Mitchell soaked it up when she wrote the lyrics to her song "Carey" here in 1970: "The wind is in from Africa. Last night I couldn't sleep. Oh, you know it sure is hard to leave here, Carey." And fellow musician Chris Rea came up with his world hit "On the Beach" on Formentera: "Upon a summer wind, there's a certain melody. Takes me back to the place that I know. On the beach…"

Surely this is the Caribbean? No, it's actually a little island in the Mediterranean.

Some mills grind slowly—even timelessly.

Ses Salines—a fascinating UNESCO World Heritage Site.

GECKO

WHERE THE CONCEPT OF TIME NO LONGER APPLIES

GECKO FORMENTERA
PLAYA DE MIGJORN
07860 CA MARÍ
+34 971 328 024
geckobeachclub.com

A hotel where guests are tempted never to leave the premises for their entire vacation—that could be the new advertising slogan for Gecko, the boutique hotel with beach club and restaurant on Migjorn Beach in Formentera. It would be a shame, because the island has a variety of attractions to offer. One is the La Mola lighthouse, which is said to have provided inspiration for Jules Verne's "Off on a Comet"; another is the Molí Vell windmill, now lovingly renovated and offering a cool respite from the summer heat. Travelers should also take the opportunity to explore the many picturesque beaches.

And yet, a vacation at the Gecko could easily be spent there and there alone. The beach restaurant is a major part of this, with a menu showcasing Mediterranean flavors and local produce while still with clear international influences: Spanish, of course, as well as Italian and seafood, Asian, and even South American cuisine. Regardless of its origin, everything tastes delicious.

At the next table, a couple is just starting their lunch with a sea view: gazpacho with vegetables from the garden, croquettes with chicken and Ibérico ham, and a wonderfully light pan de cristal ("crystal bread") with tomatoes. For the main course, she chooses pasta, tagliolini with lobster, while he goes for Asian today and enjoys stir-fried beef fillet with vegetables, soy, curry, and sweet chili.

After a lunch that stretches into the late afternoon, the couple heads to the peaceful garden to chill out on one of the Balinese canopied day beds and read a little. He heads off for a round of stand-up paddling—naturally on offer at the hotel, along with daily yoga classes.

Incidentally, they have made sure to reserve the same table for dinner.

Far left – As soon as guests arrive at the resort, they can begin switching off and recharging their mental batteries.

Left – Chef Lukas Pokorny is passionate about his job.

Below – The garden with direct beach access is a dream.

STEAK TARTARE

SERVES 4
DIFFICULTY

DRESSING
25 ml/5 tsp extra virgin olive oil
15 ml/3 tsp kimchi sauce
15 ml/3 tsp soy sauce
15 ml/3 tsp Worcestershire sauce
20 g/4 tsp tomato ketchup (preferably Heinz)
30 g/1 oz red onion
12 g/1 tbsp dashi
2 g/½ tsp Dijon mustard
2 g/½ tsp coarse sweet mustard
2 g/½ tsp HP sauce

TARTARE
600 g/1¼ lb aged Galician beef fillet
4 egg yolks
50 ml/scant ¼ cup soy sauce
40 g/1½ oz mild onions
20 g/4 tsp capers
20 g/4 tsp sweet and sour pickles
10 g/2 tsp chopped chives
100 g/4 oz soft butter
8 slices of brioche
Black pepper

GARNISH
Edible buds and flowers (optional)

1 Mix all the ingredients for the dressing in a food processor and strain through a fine sieve.

2 For the tartare, cube the meat very finely with a sharp knife, removing fat and tendons, and chill for 4 hours.

3 Mix the egg yolks and soy sauce in a bowl and chill for 4 hours.

4 Finely chop onions, capers, and pickles and slice the chives into thin rings.

5 Combine the meat with the egg yolk mixture, dressing, and chopped onions, capers, pickles, and chives. Season with black pepper.

6 Melt butter in a pan and toast the brioche slices on both sides. Top with the tartare and serve, garnished with edible buds and flowers if desired.

BAILEYS TORRIJA

SERVES 4
DIFFICULTY
✹✹☼

150 g/5⅓ oz whipped cream
150 ml/generous ½ cup milk
150 ml/generous ½ cup coconut milk
1 vanilla pod
20 ml/4 tsp Baileys
150 g/5⅓ oz white chocolate
4 slices of brioche (2 cm/1 inch thick)
150 g/5⅓ oz brown sugar

GARNISH
4 scoops of pistachio ice cream
100 g/4 oz red berries
4 sprigs of mint

1 Place cream, milk, and coconut milk in a small saucepan. Slice the vanilla pod lengthwise, scrape out the seeds, and add. Heat for 2 minutes, stirring continuously.

2 Turn off the stove, add the Baileys and the white chocolate, and let the chocolate melt. Cool to 50°C.

3 Lay the brioche slices side by side in a deep plate and pour the mixture over them. Chill for at least 6 hours.

4 Sprinkle each slice with brown sugar and caramelize it to a golden brown with a kitchen blowtorch, or toast it in a pan with butter and brown sugar until golden brown.

5 Plate up the torrijas and serve garnished with a scoop of pistachio ice cream, red berries, and mint.

QUIMERA

COOKING AS AN EXPRESSION OF JOY

QUIMERA
AV. MEDITERRÀNIA, 24
07870 LA SAVINA
+34 971 322 279
quimerarestaurant.com

A

Ana Jiménez Garcia takes whatever the garden and the sea have to offer and lets her creativity run wild. She uses both traditional and trendy cooking techniques—her toolkit as a Barcelona-born chef, always guided by the joy of doing what she loves. Garcia actually came to Formentera as a tourist and stayed on as a waitress for a summer. Now she has become a culinary reference point for the island. At Quimera—a restaurant in La Savina, just a few meters from the harbor—she embraces her Mediterranean roots. The vegetable garden set up by the restaurant's owners, who also run the legendary Hostal La Savina that has welcomed travelers since 1959, is at her disposal; 12,000 square meters (130,000 square feet), almost three acres, of supremely fertile soil, where everything is grown wholly organically. It's part of the Terra Viva Ibiza project, aiming to create a sustainable and healthy agricultural system where food is grown without synthetic chemicals, natural cycles and biodiversity are respected, and soil health is improved. For her, the garden is a resource à la carte.

"I love grandma-style dishes, as I call them. They're authentic and make you feel good," says Garcia. Simple words that sum up her art—which brought her to the attention of the *Michelin Guide*. It can be tasted in exciting combinations like braised garden carrots with cream and spiced consommé, or a whole medley of beetroot: sliced, pickled, with figs and ricotta on a lake of cold beetroot cream. The carpaccio of red Formentera prawns with mango, lime, and pistachio salt reveal the depth of Garcia's artistry. Guests at the front table are being served Galician blond beef sirloin with seasonal vegetables, blue cheese, and quince jelly, plus chicken cannelloni in organic red wine with plums and pine nuts. The only competition for your attention is the sunset—and the food wins.

"Cooking is a language you can use to express harmony, creativity, joy, or beauty. It's a universal language everyone understands," says Garcia. If you want to enjoy this pleasure for more than just one evening, stay overnight at the hostal that's part of the restaurant—and look forward to breakfast!

Links – Seafood is handled expertly here.

Below – The *Michelin Guide* also has the cuisine here in view.

Bottom – Ana Jiménez Garcia's inspiration comes from the head and the heart.

SHRIMP CARPACCIO WITH MANGO CREAM

SERVES 2–3
DIFFICULTY

CARPACCIO
6 red shrimp (prawns)

LIME CREAM
3 limes
250 g/1 cup organic cane sugar

MANGO CREAM
1 mango
Lime juice

VERMOUTH REDUCTION
750 ml/generous 3 cups red vermouth

PISTACHIO SALT
1 handful of pistachio kernels
250 g/1 cup salt

TO SERVE
Extra virgin olive oil
Red mullet roe
Sea salt flakes and pepper

1 For the carpaccio, peel the shrimp and remove the heads. Make a small cut along the back and take out the vein. Spread out a piece of parchment or baking paper on the work surface, lay the shrimp on their right side, and fold the left side of the paper over them. Press down to flatten them and freeze for 5 minutes.

2 For the lime cream, peel 2 limes (discard the peel) and prick 1 lime all over with a fork. Place everything in a small saucepan, cover with water, and add the cane sugar. Cook over very low heat until the peel is very soft. Blend the limes and 10% of the cooking water in a Thermomix until completely smooth, strain through a fine sieve, and cool. Fill a piping bag with the mixture and chill.

3 For the mango cream, peel and pit the mango, then blend the flesh in a Thermomix with a splash of lime juice. Fill a piping bag with the mixture andchill.

4 For the vermouth reduction, simmer the vermouth in a saucepan over very low heat until reduced by about half and caramelized. Pour into a bottle and cool.

5 For the pistachio salt, chop the pistachios, mix with a pinch of salt, and dry on a baking tray in the oven at 140°C/275°F (top/bottom heat) for 8 minutes. Cool and use like regular salt.

6 Spread the vermouth reduction on a plate, take the frozen shrimp out of the freezer, and quickly lay them on top. Brush with oil and sprinkle with a little pepper. Pipe three dots of lime cream and two dots of mango cream onto each shrimp. Garnish with red mullet roe, pistachio salt, and olive oil, and sprinkle with salt flakes if desired.

SCALLOPS WITH CAULIFLOWER

SERVES 1
DIFFICULTY
✷✷✷

CAULIFLOWER EMULSION
200 g/7 oz cauliflower florets
1 tsp ghee
400 ml/1¾ cups almond milk
20 g/1 oz white block chocolate
Salt

LAVENDER
95 g/scant 3½ oz ghee
5 g/1 tsp dried lavender flowers or 2 drops lavender essence
Juice of ½ lime

PARMESAN CRISP
1 piece Parmesan (about 150 g/5½ oz)

MARCONA ALMONDS
50 g/2 oz Marcona almonds (or regular almonds)
Extra virgin olive oil
Salt

SCALLOPS
4 scallops (size M or L)
Melted ghee
Salt and pepper

1 For the cauliflower emulsion, heat ghee in a small pot and lightly sauté the cauliflower florets. Add the almond milk, cover, and cook on low heat until evaporated. Puree the hot cauliflower with the chocolate in a food processor, season with salt, and set aside.

2 For the lavender, melt ghee in a small pot or pan over low heat, add the lavender, and pour in the lime juice before the lavender turns brown. Remove from the heat, strain, and keep warm.

3 For the Parmesan crisp, grate the Parmesan. Place a small amount on a sheet pan lined with parchment paper and bake in the oven at 180°C/350°F. Remove from the oven and cool.

4 For the Marcona almonds, roughly chop the almonds and roast in a pan with a little oil and salt over low heat or in the oven at 180°C/350°F for 3 minutes. Remove from the pan or oven and cool.

5 For the scallops, heat a pan until very hot. Season the scallops with salt and pepper and sear them over high heat. As soon as a crust forms, turn the scallops over and immediately pour over a little ghee. Keep frying for 1 more minute until a crust forms on the other side, and remove from the pan while still almost raw inside.

6 Spoon the cauliflower emulsion onto a large plate in 4 little mounds. Place the scallops on top and drizzle each with a little hot lavender ghee. Top with the Parmesan crisp and serve scattered with almonds.

FORMENTERA

1 JUAN Y ANDREA

A setting that's almost kitschy, but not because of any fancy decor—just thanks to the amazing location. The beach restaurant Juan y Andrea sits on the famous Playa de Ses Illetes. Palm trees line the way to the shady terrace, and with your feet in the sand, well-heeled guests enjoy the fruits of the sea. One of the most popular dishes is lobster in garlic sauce.
juanyandrea.com

2 EL PECADOR

In 2024, Catalan culinary genius Nandy Jubany opened his restaurant on the road to La Mola with a bang. He describes it as a temple of indulgence, where willpower has no sway and gluttony takes precedence. He promises delicious delicacies, elixirs, impressive company, and generally unforgettable sensory experiences—all served in a variety of extensive menus.
pecadorfor mentera.com

3 MAJORAL

Back in the 70s, Formentera was a source of inspiration for craftsmen, artisans, artists, and creative minds from all over the world. Enric Majoral also came to the island then to bask in its paradise. A self-taught artist, he started making jewelry and experimenting with different techniques. Today his beautiful creations always reflect the island's natural beauty. Explore and buy them in his minimalist, open showroom. ***majoral.com/es***

4 EL TIBURON

In the northwest, at the picturesque (and Instagrammable) Playa de Ses Illetes, El Tiburon ("The Shark") also vies for the favor of international visitors. Those who are enticed dine directly by the sea, on the shaded terrace overlooking the yachts at anchor. The menu features Mediterranean dishes, with anchovies, tuna tartare, garlic shrimp, and surf & turf. Water babies take a long dip beforehand and come along in the evening, order a cocktail that captures the essence of sunshine, and only set it down to slurp an oyster. Here's to life, salty and sweet.
tiburonformentera.com

5 LAS BRISAS

The little shop with the cool wooden door and handpicked selection of men's and women's wear is run by a uniquely characterful couple. There's the Rude Rider collection, a Palm Beach jacket, Jamin Puech bags, leather jackets from Never Enough, pants from Transit, Giorgio Brato leather shirts, vintage one-offs—and everything is displayed so you can just reach for your favorite. Can't decide? Ask for some reliable advice. ***instagram.com/lasbri sas_formentera***

CASA FORMENTERA 6

Playa Migjorn is home to a building that could have been made for this very spot. In shades of brown, it reflects its surroundings, and the eclectic rooms at Casa Formentera are popular for couples treating themselves to a break. The staff are extremely friendly and make sure everyone feels at home. The beach restaurant keeps things simple, but at a high level: terrace, wooden tables, a view, and a journey through flavors of original, unpretentious, authentic food. Who knew "no frills" could be this great?
casaformentera.com

SER-
VICE

BETTER SEX ON THE BEACH

than sand in the drink

Everything could all be so simple … My feet caress the warm sand, my eyes follow the sparkle of the water here and there, and the ebb and flow of the waves lulls me. Snippets of Spanish drift past on the breeze, mingling with the lounge music next door. Lazily, I sit up on my sun lounger. The umbrella is perfectly positioned to give me the perfect amount of shade. On my knees rests the thriller I intended to read, but can't get into. The competition is just too tempting; the beauty of Ibiza's beaches—and the beauties on those beaches—are far too distracting. And rightly so! This is the place to live and let live.
Here's my small selection out of many: eleven beaches for every taste.

CALA VADELLA

This seaside resort in the west is popular with families in summer; its wide, sandy beach remains pleasantly flat, and children can be well looked after in one of the pleasant restaurants whenever they are hungry or thirsty. It's best to park a little above the bay, take in the full view, and walk the last few meters. It's also a great place for activities, on both land and water—with pedalos, kayaking, and standup paddleboarding; however, they all take place outside the designated swimming area, to avoid clashes with swimmers or children splashing around.

BENIRRÀS

Seekers of meaning in life are often convinced they will find it on this beach in the north. However, they must accept that the journey to their chosen destination takes time, leading over several hills until the road winds down into the valley at the end. The reward is a small cove with a pebble beach, framed by cliffs on both sides. One particularly fascinating formation within clear view is known as Cap Bernat or "God's Finger." Note that the sea bed is also rocky, which is why the water is clear and ideal for snorkeling. However, swimmers should be careful not to step on sea urchins when wading in. On Sundays, like-minded people gather here for drumming sessions, light fires, and celebrate their spirituality.

LAS SALINAS

Hedonists are drawn to the south, because Las Salinas has everything the heart desires: sandy beaches, crystalline waters, chill vibes, beach bars, music, drinks—in short: fun. The Jockey Club always whips up a party with a DJ, cocktail bar, and Mediterranean food. Sa Trinxa is more laid-back. Winter travelers, take note: January 1st is when the party people meet at Las Salinas to toast the New Year with cava. Every hour on the hour, people traditionally rush into the sea to wash off the old year. Most only make it into the knee-deep shallows, but that doesn't spoil the fun.

←

CALA SAN VINCENTE

Is there a time machine to whisk you from your hotel room to Cala San Vicente in half an hour? The 30-meter-wide beach, with its fine beige sand fringing the expanse of azure water, has all the hallmarks of a classic postcard picture. Nowadays, postcards are usually left to the nostalgia mavens, and they feel very much at home on one of the comfortable sun loungers against the whitewashed classic family hotels on the bay to the northeast. The 380-meter length is perfect for swimming, so you'll have earned your iced tea afterwards.

CALA SAONA, FORMENTERA

The turquoise water is breathtaking against the reddish earth of Formentera's west coast.
Cala Saona is known as a gem, with a sandy beach hidden among the cliffs. Fans arrive at La Savina harbor in the morning by ferry, rent a bike, and ride through the pine forests along dry stone walls. They pass the time on stand-up paddleboards, heading out to the underwater caves at Punta Rasa, and stay around after their quick excursion until sunset, when the whole scene is bathed in a sea of vibrant colors.

CALA XARRACA

This bay is as unspoiled as you would imagine a bay in Ibiza's rugged north to be. It can only be reached via a path that winds through a pine forest. Down on the rocks, a Spanish woman in her twenties spreads out her beach towel and plays with her baby, while the father climbs the cliffs and displays his impressively gleaming torso from the heights. Young men swim out to a rock that seems to have been spat into the water by some ancient god, climb it with showy bravura, and outdo each other with headfirst dives into the topaz-colored water. The beach bar has also remained unspoiled and offers some beach classics alongside patatas bravas and piementos de Padrón.

TALAMANCA

Just 15 minutes' walk from Ibiza Town is a meeting-place for dancers, DJs, and cool couples with kids who are so adorably cheeky that they could only have been conceived during a night on the beach. Talamanca has several great beach restaurants, some of which are even open in the off-season. At those times you can stroll past piles of seaweed, find shells washed up by the winter waves, and watch the next generation of Spanish footballers showing off their ball skills.

ES CAVALLET

This dune-fringed spot is a favorite with people who love to show off their toned, trained luxury bodies. The often impressive waves are perfect for muscular windsurfers, too. The view from Es Cavallet in the south is extensive, all the way to Ibiza Town on one side and to Formentera on the other. The beach has a tradition of nude bathing, and the naturist section at the southern end blends into a gay scene with the legendary Chiringay beach bar as the hotspot. At the northern end, the "beautiful people" gather at El Chiringuito for long, lazy lunches. The days here can repeat endlessly. But even in the quiet off-season, the dunes and broad sandy beach have an alluring charm all their own.

CALA SALADA

Cala Salada in the west still feels pretty untouched by the summer crowds that take it over every year. Sheltered by lush pine forests, it's also a favorite spot for boat owners, who approach from the other side. The little bay fills up fast, so many people move to the cliffs that enclose it and slope down to the sea. The cool kids jump down from the rocks into a few meters of refreshing water.

PLATJA DEN BOSSA

In the height of summer, this is only the place for you if loud, hot, and sexy is your thing. A succession of beach clubs, with guys from all over the world looking to party with the right girls. On this sandy beach near Ibiza Town, Ushuaïa and the Hard Rock Hotel tower up to the sky—hotspots for daytime pool parties. Vacationers head home from Platja den Bossa with the famous "Ibiza jetlag." In winter, it's more about dog owners and walkers, and the beautiful expanse of sandy beach, flanked by a watchtower on one side and the cathedral on the other.

AGUAS BLANCAS

The former hippie favorite of Ibiza has remained an iconic destination. At Aguas Blancas, each new day dawning can be greeted with all the senses as the sun rises dramatically over the rocks in the early morning. This northeast beach is popular with locals, but never overcrowded even in August due to its steep access. Swim in your bikini—or nothing at all. Unfortunately, the beach is closed at the time of writing because the clay cliffs on either side have been severely damaged by storms and first need to be reinforced.

24/7

It's an endless succession, one superlative after another: the hottest DJs, the most lavish stages, the most modern sound systems, the sexiest dancers, the most awesome shows. If you're going to party, do it right—and that means Ibiza. Beach and open-air club parties kick off in the afternoon and continue until 11 p.m., but rarely end then; that's when the night is just getting started. Day turns into night, night turns into day. All that matters is the mood and the vibe. To help you get your bearings, I spent a week checking out a different club every day. Here are the magnificent seven.

CHINOIS

This exclusive club in Marina Botafoch aims to mix old-school hospitality with the hottest music acts to entertain its discerning guests. Over 3,000 square meters, they dance and drink in an elegant, exotic atmosphere. The opulence is all-enveloping, the perfect setting for residencies like Boho Goes Beyond, Luciano with Cadenza, and Trip.
clubchinoisibiza.com

DESTINO

Destino Pacha Resort, on the cliffs of Cap Martinet, works its magnetism all summer long, with open-air parties that are well worth checking out. For non-hotel guests with tickets, Destino runs a shuttle bus with stops including the marina in Ibiza Town. The outdoor party ends at 11 p.m., when VIPs and lucky guests keep going underground at Tox.
destinopacha.com/ibiza

PACHA

Pacha is nothing less than a club legend. Although the world has changed since it opened in 1973, night owls still flock here every night, dancing around the DJ and letting the amazing shows fire up their imagination. Pick whatever theme you're in the mood for: Music On, Pure Pacha, Flower Power … As a souvenir, take away the club's sexy cherry logo on bikinis, t-shirts, socks, and accessories. Or even dress up the kids to match. ***pacha.com***

AMNESIA

The global temple of electronic music is located in San Rafael and is packed with fans from near and far. Its parties have tempting names like "Do Not Sleep," "Boiler Room," "He. She. They.," "The Masquerade by Clytone," "Pyramid," and "Paradise." Follow the white rabbit for an amazing experience. And if amnesia hits when you wake up the next day, don't worry. Every year, the club offers new chances to make unforgettable memories. ***amnesia.es***

DC-10

If you name yourself after a jumbo jet, you must really want to be a high flyer. The underground nightclub DC-10 launched 30 years ago and is still the go-to center for all things techno. The most unforgettable experience is entering the "unhallowed halls" near the airport for Circoloco, one of Ibiza's most notorious parties. The line-up: underground talent with established artists. The mantra: everyone comes together on the dancefloor, united by music. No distractions, no decorations, no frills—just clubbing pure and simple. ***dc10ibiza.com***

HÏ

The self-proclaimed "technologically most advanced club on the planet" promises great things. And delivers on those promises night after night, with a luxurious all-new setting and, of course, star DJs. In recent years, Hï has been voted the world's best club by visitors several times. Calling these events "parties" hardly does them justice; music artists, light design, sound galaxies, and performers all come together for an unforgettable show—and all you need is a ticket to be part of it. ***hiibiza.com***

USHUAÏA

The best daytime parties, right by the sea at Playa d'en Bossa. Ushuaïa Ibiza is regularly voted the number 1 outdoor dancefloor. Hardcore fans simply stay overnight at the hotel. The DJ line-up is a Who's Who of the scene: David Guetta, Dimitri Vegas & Like Mike, Martin Garrix, Calvin Harris, Andrea Oliva, Armin Van Buuren, Swedish House Mafia. But the outdoor party stops at 11 p.m. ***theushuaia experience.com/de***

THE BUCKET-LIST

Actually, it would be possible to chill for weeks on Ibiza (see the best beaches and bays from page 218). But even if you're the type who gets bored of doing nothing, the island has plenty in store for you. Attention all go-getters: "To do or not to do? That is the question."

CATAMARAN TOUR

Gain a whole new perspective on the world from a different element—such as a catamaran tour from Ibiza to Formentera, or a sailing trip around Es Vedrá, the uninhabited rock off the west coast. The friendly and skilled team at C11 has been showered with "favorite" and "best" awards from customers for years. Book day or half-day trips, or even a two-hour sunset trip. ***charterseleven.com/en***

NAMASTE

Many people believe Ibiza has a unique healing energy. Either way, the island is a magnet for all kinds of holistic therapies and wellness trends, so virtually everyone feels in good hands here. Jeremie Quidu is the go-to for yogis seeking a journey for body, mind, and soul on their vacation. A retreat with him is the most powerful way to experience sound meditation, crystal therapy, and healing circles combined with Kundalini yoga and breathwork. ***jeremiequidu.com***

TIME AND SPACE

When the founder of the magical Cirque du Soleil commissions a piece from artist Andrew Rogers, it becomes a manifestation of thought-provoking ideas. Located on a cliff in the west, the 2014 installation—a 20-meter tower surrounded by 13 columns—symbolizes the solar system. Adjacent to it is the complementary Las Puertas de Can Sollei. These two "doors to nowhere," standing alone in an open field, may not look like much at first. But come closer, and intricate carvings and a beautiful mosaic are revealed in these artworks that obliterate time and space for a brief moment.

CAVE ADVENTUR

In the north near San Miguel, the Cueva de Can Marçà was formed over 100,000 years ago by tectonic shifts. Before heading underground, take a moment to enjoy the view from the platform at the cave entrance. This natural attraction, once a smuggler's hideout, is great for families, with a tour that leads past waterfalls, small lakes, stalactites, and stalagmites. Back in the daylight, finish your trip with a walk along the nearby cliffs.

DALT VILA AND THE CATHEDRAL

Dalt Vila (the Upper Town), the district inside Ibiza Town's mighty walls, has been a UNESCO World Heritage Site since 1999 and is a worthwhile experience. Walk through one of the three gates (I usually take the impressive main gate and the stone ramp) and stroll the narrow cobbled lanes, and you'll eventually find yourself on the hill with a panoramic view over the city and harbor. Up there is the cathedral, which has been rebuilt and changed over the centuries in the style of each new era. Next door is the archaeological museum, but you can also soak up the history of Dalt Vila simply by walking around; multilingual information panels along the paths explain its past. For the full experience, the best way down is through the Portal Nou, which leads from behind Plaza del Parque into the old town.

BIKE TOUR

An electric mountain bike or gravel bike and a group of cool people is a great way to explore the island's hills. The scenic routes lead along the coast or through the countryside, but always past Ibiza's most beautiful spots. Bike Ibiza offers bikes for rent as well as organized tours. ***bike-ibiza.com***

HIKING TOGETHER

The Hike Station was founded in 2020 by Swiss native Manuel Ehrensperger, who stumbled upon the island's long-forgotten farmers' and fishermen's paths during his daily hikes. What started as a personal passion turned into a business. Since then, he and his multilingual international team have been helping others discover Ibiza's unspoilt landscape and wild natural beauty. Manuel's motto is: "The most dangerous place in the world is your comfort zone." Take three hours and immerse yourself in a holistic hiking experience designed to boost mind, heart, and body. Every hike is different, but one thing stays the same: seven minutes of silence to meditate in and with nature.
bizahikestation.com

HORSEBACK RIDE

Mountain (well, hill, anyway) or beach, a whole new perspective can be gained from horseback. Riders of all skill levels can book a guided excursion with Ibiza Stud. As its slogan promises, the ranch in the heart of Ibiza has been the starting point for "the ride of your life" countless times. Book solo or group rides via direct message.
instagram.com/ibiza.stud

TAKE ME AWAY TO A BEAUTIFUL PLACE

Movie buffs and art lovers can't agree on whether the best outdoor meal setting is the picnic scene in "To Catch A Thief" with Grace Kelly and Cary Grant, or "Le Déjeuner sur l'Herbe" by Claude Monet. Personally, I'm torn, but in the end, I go for the movie icon over the French impressionist. Ibiza also has plenty of perfect picnic spots—just settle down on one of the many beautiful (and flat) patches of sand or earth and enjoy your food. Artfully stacked sandwiches, empanadas, Spanish pastries stuffed with all sorts of goodies, warm vegetables, fruit salad, wraps—the best part is that someone else makes it all for you. I've tasted my way through a host of take-aways, beach shacks, food trucks, and market stalls, and here's my verdict, piping hot just for you.

PICADELI

Three different salads—beetroot with orange fillets, shaved fennel with crumbled feta, broccoli with almond slivers—are handed to me in a cardboard box. The next box has Caesar salad, quinoa with cubed vegetables, and slices of grilled zucchini. There's also the soup of the day in a cup with a few slices of seeded bread. The Picadeli take-away at the edge of Santa Gertrudis is a must for foodies who like an easy life. Some stop by for the huge, ever-changing selection, others for the quirky, friendly staff. And others rave about the hummus and the gluten-free orange cake. If you're hungry or just craving a snack, grab a bite on the bench in front of Picadeli. There are also a few tables out the back, where even Wolfgang Joop likes to sit and enjoy a quick chat over a soup. ***instagram.com/picadelibiza***

PIRATA BUS →

Once upon a time, there was a man known as "Pirata" who ran a disco with a friend. One day, some hippies from Germany stopped by in their VW bus on their way south. They talked about their dreams of Formentera, the island with the amazing beaches, and awakened the two friends' curiosity. They followed in the wake of the hippies, bought an old bus, and parked it on Migjorn Beach as a beach bar. In the 1970s, the bus became a meeting spot for musicians and travelers, but in the 1980s, the authorities finally cracked down and made them move. The bus was lifted away by crane and replaced with a wooden shack. But the loyal guests and the enchanting atmosphere are still there today. For a chilled day at the beach, grab some simple tapas and cold drinks. The main thing is to take your time and enjoy the warmth and simplicity. The sunset waves goodbye to a 70s soundtrack. ***piratabus.com***

PASSION CAFÉ

The passion for healthy, lovingly prepared food is obvious at Passion Cafés—both for guests and staff. Lana Love came up with the idea for these "health food" cafés with a chill vibe back in 2002, and now there are four locations on the island, all hotspots for people who take care of their bodies. My favorite is the one in Marina Botafoch, where everyone seems to know everyone. Some people even go there every day after their morning workout for a protein shake and a dose of happiness in the form of a lavishly garnished açai or granola bowl, or a deluxe avocado toast. Tip: The salads, wraps, and Buddha bowls are also available in attractive take-away containers. They're perfect as a picnic spent lounging on a cotton towel at nearby Talamanca Beach, and deliver just the right energy for a game of beach volleyball afterwards.
passioncafe.com

IMPREVISTO IBIZA

Who eats at a Pizza World Championship winner's? World champs like Zinedine Zidane. The French football god knows where to go for the best. At Imprevisto in a lively part of Ibiza Town, the owners serve up outstanding pizzas made from sourdough with a mix of 100% organic flours, baked in a stone oven, and topped with products imported straight from Italy. The pizzas have tempting names like Gina (tomato, fior di latte, arugula, cherry tomatoes, burrata, bacon, olives, Parmigiano Reggiano), Tartufa (truffle cream, fior di latte, gorgonzola, burrata, arugula, Parmigiano Reggiano, truffled balsamic, crushed hazelnuts), and Queen (tomatoes, fior di latte, ham, mushrooms, basil, oregano). All of them make you wish your holiday would never end—or at least set you up for a long night of dancing. Pick up your pizza yourself to get 15% off. So here's a tip: choose your favorite for the evening, sit on a bench at Ibiza's harbor with the box on your knees, and enjoy it with a side of the views over Pacha.

MERCAT VELL

Ibiza Town's old market. Years ago, Niko the Argentinian washed up on the island and has been filling his little stand at the old market with homemade goodies every summer since. From about April to September, you'll find him under the hall roof between the columns. He'll probably have a salad or two and will happily top two slices of dark, moist bread with avocado for you. Don't miss the delicious almond or orange cake, and definitely try the fresh juices. Mercat Vell will soon be renovated and the stands will move. Keep your eyes open!

PANTASTIC

Think the little corner shop in the new town is just a bakery and expect it to sell plain bread? Think again. Pantastic attracts foodies from all over the island, even habitual carb-avoiders. And for good reason: everything from the ovens is made from stone-ground flour that locks in all the grains' goodness—no additives, stabilizers, or enzymes. You can certainly taste the difference. The tempting loaves line the shelves. Topped with vegetables or cheese, herb spread, smoked ham, or the obligatory avocado, this bread is the perfect snack. The same goes for the fragrant focaccia, packed up warm to go. If you're going to indulge, do it right: nobody can refuse the irresistible cinnamon rolls. The barista behind the counter reaches through the little window to hand out coffee made from 100% arabica beans, topped with a charming almond milk heart.
pantasticibiza.com/cafe

ARTE DE VIVIR

Ibiza has mastered the art of sweet idleness to perfection. Who would think of leaving behind the attractions of the beach, the clubs, or the countryside to wander around a museum or gallery for a few hours? But that's a shame, because the island's art is well worth your attention. I've taken a look around for you and compiled my top ten cultural highlights, for inspiring ideas of a different kind.

CAN IBIZA ART FAIR

The third edition of Contemporary Art Now (CAN) took place in June 2024. When over 30 national and international galleries fill the huge halls on the outskirts of Ibiza Town, you could almost be in Barcelona or Madrid. This innovative art fair seeks to push boundaries and showcases fresh, creatively avant-garde forms of expression, with art as a force of constant reinvention. ***contemporaryart now.com/en***

MUSEUM MACE

A pioneer displaying contemporary art since 1969 inside the old fortress walls of Ibiza Town, the Museo de Arte Contemporáneo (MACE) is one of the first of its kind in Spain and is proud of its trailblazing role as a hub for modern art. The glass building is also an architectural eye-catcher. Inside, you can admire works by local legends like Eduard Micus, Erwin Broner, "Portmany," and Antoni Tàpies.

LA NAVE SALINAS

Originally intended as a warehouse for salt or "white gold," this has been a dynamic exhibition space in the Ses Salines area since 2015. Colombian art collector and gallerist Lio Malca displays selected treasures from his collection, breaking away from the customary narratives of high art and blurring the lines between urban, popular, and academic art. Pop art by KAWS, Kenny Scharf, and Keith Haring, and media art by Marco Brambilla have already made appearances in Ibiza. Lio Malca is firmly convinced that art brings magic and meaning to life. Why not give it a try? ***en.lanavesalinas.org***

MIRA GATHERING

Gathering in London's Soho is cool. The gallery for contemporary art, founded by Alexander Flick, always has an exhibition program with its finger on the pulse (or even a beat ahead), combining up-and-coming international voices with established names. But it's also cool because instead of expanding into another cultural metropolis, they chose Sant Miguel de Balansat. Mira Gathering (named after Alexander's daughter) is both gallery and bar, connecting art, people, music, and food in easy-going, unpretentious style. ***mirabygathering.com***

CENTRE ANTONI TUR "GABRIELET"

The bright building complex is already impressive. Formentera's arts and crafts center is housed in a former barracks in the main town of San Francesc. It was renovated and remodeled to make sure the region's important trades—both then and now—aren't forgotten, and to preserve the cultural heritage for the future. That's quite a noble goal they're pursuing here. The events in the courtyard between the buildings are also worth checking out, especially on warm summer evenings.

GALERIA TAMBIEN

Art and design come together in Galeria Tambien in Santa Gertrudis to create an eclectic overall image, curated by Natalie Rich and Jorge Fernández. The couple, whose focus is mid-century furniture and design, combine finds by Charlotte Perriand, Pierre Jeanneret, and Gio Ponti with photos, ceramics, and paintings by up-and-coming artists. "We're always on the lookout for special pieces that have a story," they explain. Their gallery is a treasure trove for iconic works and objects that buyers will connect with their own stories.
galeriatambien.com

ESPACIO MICUS

Once upon a time, German artist Eduard Micus fell in love with Ibiza, decided to stay, and built himself a studio in an old finca near Jesus. On the island, he painted poetic pictures in hues of white, gray, and beige, and started creating works with seemingly worthless things like driftwood, broken ropes, fruit crates, and the like—capturing what was available to him there. The late artist's house is now a museum, with exhibition spaces that come to life in the easy-going atmosphere. Micus's work is on display, along with solo shows by contemporary colleagues.
espacio-micus.com

ART CAFÉ CAN TIXEDO

On the road between San Antonio and Santa Gertrudis, Art Café Can Tixedo attracts fans of relaxed, communal dining, but also those who love a helping of culture with their meal. A new exhibition opens every month. If you miss it, you can "read" the walls: Local, national, and international artists have left their colorful marks here over the years.
cantixedo.com/en/#art

GALERIE PARRA & ROMERO

The Santa Gertrudis branch of the renowned Madrid gallery Parra & Romero is like a blank canvas, the perfectly austere backdrop for contemporary exhibitions straddling conceptual art and minimalism. The program is not curated for a specific medium, leaving plenty of scope for intellectual exchange. That exchange continues in the nearby warehouse, where projects interact with the location. Incidentally, a chat with gallerist Guillermo Romero Parra is both educational and entertaining. ***parra-romero.com***

ALL THE FUN OF THE MARKET

OR: HOW A CERAMIC BOWL FOUND ITSELF ON A BERBER RUG

The markets on Ibiza are for shopping—but they have plenty of other functions too. Some vendors make their living here on the island; some visitors head for a different market every day just to socialize; many simply browse for inspiration because the wares are unique, the atmosphere is usually enhanced by a live band, and the scene is always lively. Ceramics, hand-stitched shirts, healing stones, organic soaps, dyed furs—everyone finds something. No wonder the markets are a top attraction for holidaymakers.

The popular hippie markets began life in the 1960s, when hordes of hippies spent their winters in Goa, India, or Bali and brought back fabrics, scarves, stones, incense, and more to their summer home of Ibiza. They sold these pretty things at markets, quickly attracting craftspeople and artists and resulting in a great atmosphere and a quirky selection of goods. Even today, that old-school ambience can still be felt and the perfect piece of handmade jewelry can often be found. I've checked out a market for every day of the week for you.

The **Las Dalias Night Market** takes place on Mondays, Tuesdays, and Sundays. The lively hustle and bustle of this atmospheric evening market is legendary. More than 100 stalls, all chosen for their quality and originality, present fashion, jewelry, and art. There are several bars, restaurants, a tea tent, a pizza stand, a churros stall, and live music.
When: Night market in June & September from 6:00 p.m. to 11:30 p.m., July & August from 6:00 p.m. to midnight.
lasdalias.es/en/markets

Later, the night continues at the cool **Las Dalias Club**, called **Akasha**. Here, you can dive into a whole new dimension of sound. The eclectic lineup brings together different electronic music genres with both international and local talents, like Sven Väth, Stefan Obermeier, Nico Stojan, Ida Engberg, Amonita, and many more. Best way to start? Try one of the themed nights like Namaste.
akashaibiza.com

On Wednesdays during the summer season, things get lively at the **Punta Arabí Hippie Market** in the resort of Es Canár. It's a long-standing tradition and still one of the biggest markets on the island. The many stalls are spread out in the shade of pine trees between white apartment buildings and display all kinds of objects from around the world, many handmade. In the children's area, little ones can craft their own souvenirs. A range of bars and restaurants serve up drinks and snacks, while live music keeps the mood going.
When: Every Wednesday from May to October, 10:00 a.m. to 7:00 p.m.
hippymarket.info

On Thursdays, it's worth making a detour to Cala Llonga. The small **"after beach market"** there is packed with stalls of local craftspeople. Accessories and silver jewelry with gemstones are especially popular.
When: Thursdays from May to October, 6:30 p.m. to 10:00 p.m.

On Thursday evenings, the **arts and crafts market** sets up in the square in front of the church in **San Rafael**, a lovely weekly market for wares including ceramics in both traditional and modern designs.
When: Thursdays from late June to mid-September, 7:30 p.m. to 10:30 p.m.
visit.santantoni.net/de/was-tun/strassenmaerkte/kunsthandwerk-in-sant-rafel

On Fridays, **arts and crafts** take center stage in **Santa Gertrudis**. Local artists show off their work, from paintings and jewelry to crocheted baby shoes. The stalls on the village square are surrounded by restaurants and bars, so there's plenty to whet the appetite. Children have fun too—they can play right next door at the playground behind the church.
When: Every Friday from late May to September, 7:00 p.m. to midnight.

The **Mercadillo Sant Jordi** on Saturdays is irresistible. The flea market at the old racetrack near the airport is popular with locals, too, as a place to find pretty much anything—and at a fair price (haggling allowed). After your secondhand shopping, enjoy a cortado on the terrace and you'll probably catch a spontaneous jam session.
When: Every Saturday, all year round, from 8:00 a.m. to 3:00 p.m.
mercadillodesantjordi.com

The **organic and arts & crafts market in San José** also takes place on Saturdays. Here, Ibiza's traditions are alive and well. Some stalls are filled with fruit, vegetables, and pastries, while others offer all kinds of handmade crafts. Inspired? Seek out a workshop—there's everything from bread baking to composting to learn about.
When: Saturdays from June to October, 9:30 a.m. to 1:30 p.m.
santjosep.net/nl/traditionelles-ibizenkisches-kunsthandwerk

On Sundays the market scene heads north, specifically to the **arts and crafts market in San Juan**. Alongside homemade cakes, vegan sandwiches, island coffee, and organic vegetables, there are local crafts (my tip: check out the delicate rings, key fobs with beads and bells, and the Mexican Día de Muertos souvenirs), plus plenty of shirts, skirts, dresses, and fur jackets to stash in your new recycled-fabric shopping bag. From midday, live bands play on the steps to the village square, getting both locals and visitors grooving.
When: Every Sunday, all year round, 9:00 a.m. to 4:00 p.m.

On Sundays and Wednesdays during the season, you can pick up beautiful or practical things from artisans at Formentera's **biggest market**. With live music and plentiful bars all around, El Pilar de la Mola, at the southern tip of the island, turns into a lively cultural hotspot where crafters, sellers, and curious visitors all come together.
When: Wednesdays and Sundays, May to October, 4:30 p.m. to 10:00 p.m.

INDEX

CALLWEY

Books make you happy

since

1884

Since its founding, Callwey Verlag has become one of Germany's leading publishers, known for its high-quality books on architecture, design, gardening, living, and lifestyle. What started over 140 years ago with Georg D.W. Callwey opening a publishing bookstore quickly grew into a renowned publishing house that has inspired generations of readers.
The fourth generation now continues the legacy with the same dedication and innovative spirit that drove the founders.

Callwey Verlag stands for inspiration, creativity, and top quality. Every book that leaves the publishing house is a masterpiece in its own right, often planned and developed over years, carefully curated, designed, and lovingly crafted with the best papers – nothing has changed about that since 1884.

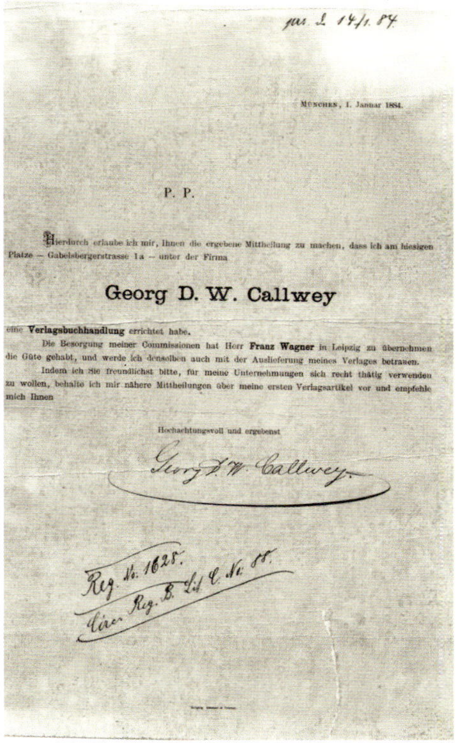

MÜNCHEN, 1. Januar 1884.

P. P.

Hierdurch erlaube ich mir, Ihnen die ergebene Mittheilung zu machen, dass ich am hiesigen Platze – Gabelsbergerstrasse 1a – unter der Firma

Georg D. W. Callwey

eine **Verlagsbuchhandlung** errichtet habe.

Die Besorgung meiner Commissionen hat Herr **Franz Wagner** in Leipzig zu übernehmen die Güte gehabt, und werde ich denselben auch mit der Auslieferung meines Verlages betrauen.

Indem ich Sie freundlichst bitte, für meine Unternehmungen sich recht thätig verwenden zu wollen, behalte ich mir nähere Mittheilungen über meine ersten Verlagsartikel vor und empfehle mich Ihnen

Hochachtungsvoll und ergebenst

Georg D. W. Callwey

A journey through the centuries: The historic publishing offices, staff from the 1920s and 1960s, the publishing founder Georg D.W. Callwey, and members of the publisher's family, including Marcella Prior-Callwey.

IMPRINT

CALLWEY 1884

© 2026 CALLWEY GMBH
KLENZESTRASSE 36
80469 MÜNCHEN
buch@callwey.de
+49 89 8905080-0
www.callwey.de

See you on Instagram:
www.instagram.com/callwey

ISBN 978-3-7667-2869-2
1st edition 2026

BIBLIOGRAPHIC INFORMATION FROM THE GERMAN NATIONAL LIBRARY
The German National Library lists this publication in the German National Bibliography; detailed bibliographic data can be found online at dnb.d-nb.de.

WE HOPE YOU ENJOY THIS BOOK!
Author: Sherin Kneifl
Project lead: Anna Seidel
Photographer: Luana Failla
Translation: Callwey Editorial Team
Translation editing: Alison Moffat-McLynn
Design & typesetting: Sina Preuße
Production: Oliver Meier

THE AUTHOR:
Sherin Kneifl knows how to shine a light on exciting stories. As a journalist, she has written for renowned media including *BUNTE*, *ELLE*, *InStyle*, and the *Süddeutsche Zeitung*. As editor-in-chief of Swiss lifestyle and fashion magazines *Style* and *Bolero*, she always hit the right note – a talent she has drawn on for *A Guest In Ibiza*.

THE PHOTOGRAPHER:
Luana Failla is from Sicily and currently lives in Ibiza. She has been a food photographer all over Europe for almost ten years, with work published in magazines including *Tapas Magazine*, *White Ibiza*, *Esquire*, *Condé Nast Traveller*, *Forbes*, and *Salvaje*, to name but a few. A fine arts graduate, she has a strong visual understanding and a profoundly intuitive approach to working with colors, light, and composition.

OTHER PHOTOGRAPHS:
Adobe Stock, p.: 17 (l.), 52–53, 55, 66–67, 68–69, 94, 98–99, 100, 101 (l.), 142–145, 198–199, 200 (top)
Unsplash: p. 4 (Monique) / **pp. 12–13** (Getty Images) / **p. 16** (Oliver Thomas) / **p. 17** (top r./ Ferran Feixas) / **p. 17** (bottom r./Bjorn Agerbeek) / **p. 48** (Caroline Hernandez) / **p. 49** (Jonathan Borba) / **p. 62** (Valerie Vaillancourt) / **p. 224** (Jonathan Photography/Melanie Maya) / **p. 101** (r./Florian Settele; bottom l./ Tess van den Eeckhout)
iStock: p. 200 (b./Lunamarina) / **p. 201** (Luna marina, Martin Silva Cosentino, photovideo stock) / **p. 218** (Eivaisla) / **p. 219** (top center/Luna marina) / **p. 219** (Davide Zanin) / **p. 220** (jon11/ Jürgen Sack/thanasus) / **p. 221** (jotapg/Javier Duran) / **p. 223** (Valery Ambartsumian) / **p. 225** (FGM/Ian McDonnell) / **p. 226** (Ohla Afanesieva/Ildar Abulkhanov) / **p. 227** (jotapg/Ziga Plahutar) / **p. 228** (Artesia Wells) / **p. 230** (Brian Holm Nielsen) / **p. 231** (olgakr) / **p. 234** (amoklv)
PR: p. 48: ©La Torre del Canonigo (@latorre delcanonigo), ©Teatro Pereyra (@teatropereyra ibiza1898) / **p. 49:** ©Noss (@nossibiza) / **p. 62:** ©Maria B. Ceramics (@mariab.ceramics) / **p. 63:** ©Tropicana (@tropicana_ibiza), ©El Chi ringuito (@elchiringuito_ibiza), ©Casa Maca (@casamacaibiza), ©Jul's Restaurant (@juls ibiza) / **p. 94:** ©Es Tragón (@estragonibiza), ©Sa Capella (@sacapellaibiza) / p. 95: Ibiza Rocks ©Elliot Young, ©Hotel Oku Ibiza (@okuhotels), ©O Beach Ibiza (@obeachibiza) / **p. 138:** ©El Silencio (@elsilencioibiza), ©Cotton Beach Club (@cottonbeachclub), ©Es Torrent (@estorrent restaurant), **p. 139:** ©Urusuai (@urusai.ibiza), ©Six Senses Ibiza (@sixsenses.ibiza), ©Obsolete (@obsolete_ibiza) / **p. 194:** ©Gatzara Suties (@hotelgatzaraibiza), ©Meke (@mekecoffee ibiza), La Galeria Elefante ©Gypsy Westwood (@ lagaleriaelefanteibiza) / **p. 195:** ©Macao Café (@macaocafesantagertrudis), ©Chez Bibi (@ chez_ bibi_von_bakery_ibiza), ©Siempre (@ siempre_deco_ibiza) / **p. 214:** ©Juan Y Andrea (@juan yandreaoficial), ©Majoral (@majoral-jewelry), ©El Pecador (@pecador_formentera) / **p. 215:** ©El Tiburon (@tiburonformentera_ beachclub), ©Las Brisas (@lasbrisas_formentera), ©Casa Formentera (@casaformentera) / **p. 222** (top to bottom): Chinois ©Mario Pina (@ chinoisibiza), Destino ©Julian Farina, Tatiana Chausovsky (@destin opachaofficial) / **p. 223:** ©Ushuaïa Ibiza Beach Hotel (@ushuaiaibiza) / **p. 227** (l. to r.): ©Passion Café (@passioncafe) / **p. 228:** ©Mira Gathering (@mira.gathering.ibiza) / **p. 229** (top to bottom): Centre Antoni Tur Gabrielet ©Marià Castelló, ©Galerie Parra & Romero, ©Galeria Tambien.

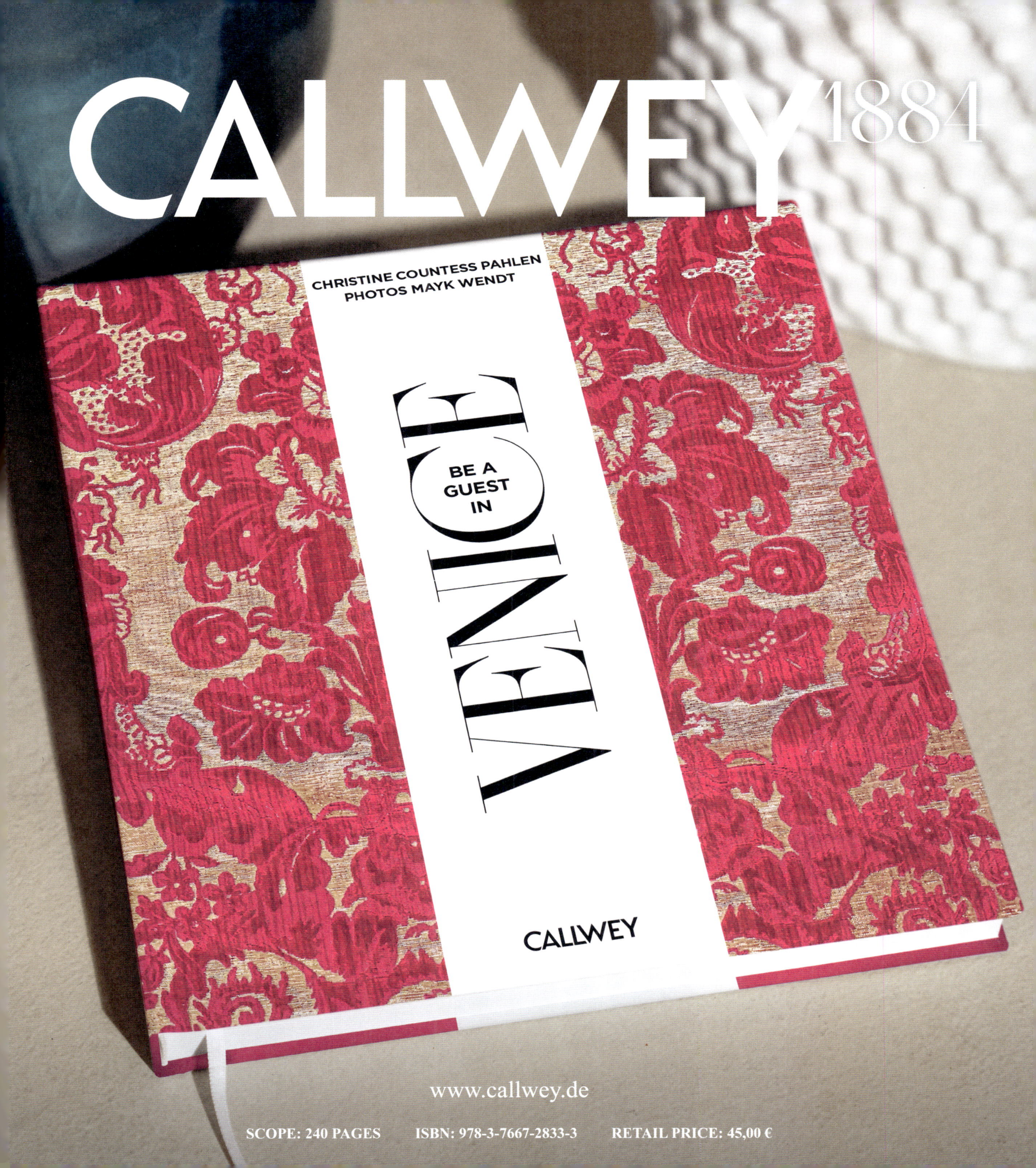
CALLWEY 1884
CHRISTINE COUNTESS PAHLEN
PHOTOS MAYK WENDT
BE A GUEST IN
VENICE
CALLWEY
www.callwey.de
SCOPE: 240 PAGES
ISBN: 978-3-7667-2833-3
RETAIL PRICE: 45,00 €